Table Of Contents

Introduction..5
Overview...10
Getting to Newfoundland & Labrador...............11
   By Air..11
   By Sea...17
   By Land...23
Planning Your Trip...37
Must-See Attractions..47
The East Coast Trail...70
Gros Morne National Park....................................74
Labrador..79
Activities and Adventures....................................84
Indigenous Groups Newfoundland and Labrador. 93
The Vibrant Communities of Newfoundland & Labrador... 97
   Western Region & Northern Peninsula........... 97
      Port aux Basques.......................................98
      Corner Brook..100
      Rocky Harbour (Gros Morne)...................103
      Norris Point (Gros Morne).......................106
      Woody Point (Gros Morne)......................109
      Bonne Bay (Gros Morne)........................112
      Cow Head (Gros Morne).........................115
      Woody Point (Gros Morne)......................118
      St. Anthony (Northern Peninsula)........... 121
      L'Anse aux Meadows (Viking Settlement, Northern Peninsula)................................ 124
      Deer Lake...127
   Central Region.. 130
      Twillingate... 131
      Fogo Island.. 134

  Grand Falls-Windsor................................ 137
  Gander... 140
  Terra Nova National Park........................ 142
 Eastern Region... 146
  Clarenville.. 147
  Bonavista... 149
  Trinity... 152
  Port Rexton.. 155
  Elliston... 158
  Dildo.. 160
 Avalon Peninsula.. 164
  St. John's... 165
  Cape Spear.. 167
  Quidi Vidi... 170
  Petty Harbour.. 173
  Brigus.. 175
  Cupids... 178
  Bay Bulls... 181
  Ferryland... 184
 Labrador... 187
  Happy Valley-Goose Bay......................... 188
  Labrador City/Wabush............................. 189
  Red Bay... 190
Let's Wrap It Up.. 191
 Newfoundland & Labrador Map..................... 198
Calendars...199

© 2023 by HJ Companion

Cover design: HJ Companion

Cover photograph: HJ Companion

First Edition: 2023

The copyright page is intended to protect the rights of the author and publisher and to provide important information about the book's publication. Unauthorized use or distribution of this book may result in civil and criminal penalties.

The Disclaimer Stuff....

The information provided in this travel guide to Newfoundland and Labrador is intended for general informational purposes only. While every effort has been made to ensure the accuracy and reliability of the content, we cannot guarantee that all information is up to date or completely free from errors.

Travel information, including transportation schedules, accommodation options, and attraction details, may be subject to change without prior notice. It is advisable to verify all information independently before making any travel arrangements or decisions.

The experiences and opinions shared in this guide are based on personal accounts and may vary from individual to individual. The author and publisher do not assume any responsibility for the actions, choices, or experiences of readers who rely solely on the information provided in this book.

Travel involves inherent risks, and readers are encouraged to exercise caution and undertake their own research and assessment of potential hazards before embarking on any journey. It is recommended to consult with relevant authorities, such as local tourism offices or government agencies, for the most up-to-date travel advisories, safety guidelines, and regulations.
Furthermore, this travel guide may contain references or suggestions for activities, tours, or

services provided by third-party companies or individuals. The inclusion of such information does not constitute an endorsement or recommendation by the author or publisher, and readers are encouraged to conduct their own due diligence and make independent decisions regarding these offerings.

The author and publisher disclaim any liability for any loss, injury, or inconvenience sustained by individuals or entities relying on the information provided in this travel guide. Readers are solely responsible for their own actions and decisions while traveling.

Remember to respect the environment, local customs, and laws during your travels. Always prioritize your personal safety and the well-being of those around you.

Introduction

Newfoundland & Labrador is a province in eastern Canada that is rich in history, culture, and natural beauty. From the rugged coastline of the Avalon Peninsula to the majestic peaks of the Torngat Mountains, this province has something to offer every type of traveler.

In this travel book, we will provide you with a comprehensive guide to exploring Newfoundland & Labrador. Whether you're a first-time visitor or a seasoned traveler, this book will give you all the information you need to plan an unforgettable trip.

First, we'll provide an overview of the province's geography and history, including how it became a part of Canada and the influence of Indigenous peoples on the region.

We'll also highlight some of the reasons why Newfoundland & Labrador is a unique and interesting travel destination, from its distinctive accents and traditions to its stunning natural landscapes.

Then, we'll give you an overview of what the book will cover, including transportation options, planning your trip, exploring St. John's, hiking the East Coast Trail, visiting Gros Morne National Park, exploring Labrador, engaging in activities and adventures, trying local food and drink, and practical information such as entry requirements and visa information.

By the end of this book, you'll have a comprehensive understanding of Newfoundland & Labrador and be ready to plan an unforgettable trip to this incredible province.

Brief overview of the province's geography and history

Newfoundland & Labrador is a province located in eastern Canada, bordered by Quebec to the west and the Atlantic Ocean to the east. The province is made up of two main regions: the island of Newfoundland and the mainland region of Labrador.

The geography of Newfoundland & Labrador is varied and includes rugged coastline, rolling hills, deep fjords, and towering mountains. The province is also home to numerous lakes, rivers, and forests, making it a popular destination for outdoor enthusiasts.

The history of Newfoundland & Labrador is rich and complex, dating back thousands of years. The region was originally inhabited by Indigenous peoples, including the Innu, Inuit, and Beothuk, who developed unique cultures and traditions over time.

In 1497, the region was visited by Italian explorer Giovanni Caboto (also known as John Cabot), who claimed the land for England.

Over the next several centuries, Newfoundland & Labrador became an important center for fishing and shipping, with settlements established by the French, English, and other European powers.

In the 20th century, Newfoundland & Labrador became a part of Canada, but has retained its unique culture and identity.

Today, the province is a popular destination for tourists from around the world, offering a fascinating blend of history, culture, and natural beauty.

Reasons why Newfoundland & Labrador is a unique and interesting travel destination

Newfoundland & Labrador is a destination unlike any other in the world. This province is known for its rugged coastline, stunning landscapes, and rich cultural heritage. There are several reasons why Newfoundland & Labrador is a unique and interesting travel destination:

1. Rich history and culture: Newfoundland & Labrador has a rich history and culture that is deeply intertwined with the sea. The province was a major center for fishing and shipping for centuries, and its people have developed unique traditions and ways of life that reflect this history. From the traditional music and dance of the region to its distinctive dialects and accents, Newfoundland & Labrador offers a fascinating glimpse into the culture and heritage of Atlantic Canada.

2. Natural beauty: The province is home to some of the most stunning natural landscapes in the world. From the rugged coastline of the Avalon Peninsula to the towering mountains of the Torngat Mountains National Park, Newfoundland & Labrador offers endless opportunities for outdoor exploration and adventure. Visitors can hike the East Coast Trail, go whale watching, or spot icebergs and seabirds along the coastline.

3. Unique wildlife: Newfoundland & Labrador is home to several species of wildlife that are not found anywhere else in the world. The province is famous for its population of Atlantic puffins, as well as its herds of caribou, which roam the tundra in search of food. Visitors can also see whales, dolphins, seals, and other marine life along the coastline.

4. Friendly locals: Newfoundland & Labrador is known for its friendly and welcoming locals. Visitors can expect to be greeted with a warm smile and a helping hand, as the people of the province are known for their hospitality and generosity.

5. Delicious cuisine: The cuisine of Newfoundland & Labrador is hearty and delicious, reflecting the province's history as a center for fishing and hunting. Visitors can enjoy traditional dishes such as fish and

chips, seafood chowder, and moose stew, as well as local craft beer and spirits.

Overall, Newfoundland & Labrador is a destination that offers a unique blend of history, culture, natural beauty, and hospitality. It's a place where visitors can immerse themselves in the local way of life, explore stunning landscapes, and create memories that will last a lifetime.

Overview

This book will cover various topics related to travel and tourism in the province. This could include information on:
1. Popular tourist destinations and attractions, such as national parks, museums, historical sites, and cultural events.
2. Outdoor activities and adventure sports, such as hiking, kayaking, fishing, and hunting.
3. Accommodations, dining, and transportation options for visitors to the province.
4. Local culture and traditions, including music, dance, festivals, and cuisine.
5. Practical travel tips, such as weather and climate considerations, visa requirements, and health and safety advice.

Getting to Newfoundland & Labrador

Introduction

Getting to Newfoundland & Labrador can be an adventure in itself, with options ranging from air travel to ferries and driving. Whether you're coming from another part of Canada, the United States, or an international destination, there are several ways to reach this unique and fascinating province.

In this chapter, we'll explore the various options for getting to Newfoundland & Labrador, including major airports and airlines, ferry routes and schedules, and driving tips. We'll also cover practical considerations such as weather, passport and visa requirements, and customs and immigration procedures, to help you plan your trip with confidence.

So sit back, relax, and let's dive into the many ways to get to Newfoundland & Labrador.

By Air

Newfoundland & Labrador is home to several major airports that serve both domestic and international flights. The largest airport in the province is the St. John's International Airport (YYT), located in the capital city of St. John's. With over 20 airlines offering daily flights to and from destinations across Canada, the United States, and Europe, St. John's International Airport is the gateway to Newfoundland & Labrador for many travelers.

Other major airports in the province include the Gander International Airport (YQX), located in central Newfoundland, and the Deer Lake Regional Airport (YDF), located in western Newfoundland.

These airports offer domestic flights to and from other parts of Canada, as well as seasonal flights to and from popular tourist destinations such as Toronto and Halifax.

In addition to these major airports, there are several smaller regional airports throughout Newfoundland & Labrador that offer flights to nearby destinations. These include the Stephenville International Airport (YJT), the Goose Bay Airport (YYR), and the Wabush Airport (YWK).

No matter which airport you fly into, you'll find a range of services and amenities to make your travel experience as comfortable as possible. From car rental agencies and shuttle services to restaurants and shops, these airports are well-equipped to meet the needs of travelers from around the world.

Airlines serving the province

Newfoundland & Labrador is served by several major airlines, as well as a number of smaller regional carriers. The largest airlines serving the province are Air Canada, WestJet, and Porter Airlines, all of which offer daily flights to and from major cities across Canada, such as Toronto, Montreal, and Halifax.

These airlines also offer connecting flights to international destinations in the United States and Europe, making it easy to reach Newfoundland & Labrador from almost anywhere in the world.

Other airlines serving Newfoundland & Labrador include PAL Airlines, which operates regional flights throughout the province and to nearby destinations in Atlantic Canada, and Provincial Airlines, which offers charter flights and air cargo services throughout the province.

Additionally, Air Labrador and Labrador Airways provide air services to remote communities and destinations in northern Labrador.

When booking your flights to Newfoundland & Labrador, it's important to compare prices and schedules to find the best deal.

Be sure to check for promotions and discounts, and consider booking well in advance to secure the lowest fares. Many airlines also offer loyalty programs and rewards for frequent travelers, so it's worth checking to see if you can earn points or miles for your flights to and from the province.

Flights from other Canadian cities and international destinations

Newfoundland & Labrador is easily accessible from other Canadian cities, with several major airlines offering daily flights to and from major hubs such as Toronto, Montreal, and Halifax. Air Canada, WestJet, and Porter Airlines all operate flights to St. John's International Airport from these and other Canadian cities, with multiple flights per day available.

For travelers coming from international destinations, St. John's International Airport also offers a number of direct flights to and from major cities in the United States and Europe.

American Airlines, Delta Air Lines, and United Airlines all operate direct flights to St. John's from cities such as New York, Boston, and London, while Air Canada and WestJet offer direct flights from destinations such as Dublin, Frankfurt, and Paris.

In addition to direct flights, there are also several connecting flights available from other Canadian and international cities, making it easy to reach Newfoundland & Labrador from almost anywhere in the world.

When booking your flights, be sure to check for connecting options and compare prices and schedules to find the best deal.

Keep in mind that flight schedules and availability may vary depending on the season, so it's important to plan your trip in advance and book your flights accordingly.

Additionally, it's important to check passport and visa requirements for international travelers, and to allow ample time for customs and immigration procedures upon arrival in Newfoundland & Labrador.

Tips for finding the best airfare deals

Finding the best airfare deals for your trip to Newfoundland & Labrador requires some research and savvy planning. Here are some tips to help you save money on your flights:

1. Book in advance: Generally, the earlier you book your flights, the better the deal you can find. Aim to book at least a few months in advance, especially if you're traveling during peak season.

2. Be flexible with travel dates: If you're able to be flexible with your travel dates, you may be able to find better deals. Try searching for flights on different days of the week or in

different months to see if there are any significant price differences.

3. Use comparison websites: There are several websites that allow you to compare prices from different airlines and travel providers. Use these websites to quickly find the best deals and compare prices across multiple airlines.

4. Sign up for alerts: Many airlines and travel websites offer email alerts for price drops and special promotions. Sign up for these alerts to be notified when prices drop on flights to Newfoundland & Labrador.

5. Look for promo codes and discounts: Check for promo codes and discounts on airline websites and social media pages, and be sure to use them when booking your flights.

6. Consider alternative airports: If you're flying into Newfoundland & Labrador from a nearby city or destination, consider flying into a smaller regional airport instead of a major international airport. This can often result in significant cost savings.

By using these tips and being proactive about your flight booking, you can find the best airfare deals and save money on your trip to Newfoundland & Labrador.

By Sea

Traveling to Newfoundland & Labrador by sea can be an exciting and unique way to experience the province's rugged coastlines and stunning landscapes.

There are several ferry services that connect Newfoundland & Labrador to mainland Canada and the United States, making it a convenient option for travelers looking for an alternative to flying.

In this section, we'll provide an overview of the ferry services available, as well as tips for making the most of your journey by sea.

Ferries to Newfoundland & Labrador from Nova Scotia

Marine Atlantic Ferry Service

The Marine Atlantic ferry service operates year-round, connecting North Sydney, Nova Scotia to both Port aux Basques and Argentia in Newfoundland & Labrador.

The journey from North Sydney to Port aux Basques takes approximately 6-8 hours, while the journey from North Sydney to Argentia takes approximately 14-16 hours.

The ferries offer a variety of amenities, including food service, sleeping cabins, and entertainment options.

Advance booking is recommended, especially during peak season, as the ferries can fill up quickly.

Bay Ferries Service

The Bay Ferries service operates seasonally, connecting North Sydney, Nova Scotia to Port aux Basques in Newfoundland & Labrador.

The journey takes approximately 6 hours.
The ferries offer a variety of amenities, including food service, comfortable seating, and outdoor deck areas.

Advance booking is recommended, especially during peak season.

Both of these ferry services offer a unique and scenic way to travel to Newfoundland & Labrador, and can be a great option for those who enjoy a slower pace of travel or want to bring a vehicle with them.

Additionally, the ferry journey itself can be an experience in and of itself, with stunning views of the ocean and coastline.

Routes and Schedules

To plan your journey by ferry to Newfoundland & Labrador, it's important to be aware of the various routes and schedules available.

The Marine Atlantic ferry service operates year-round and offers two routes: North Sydney, Nova Scotia to Port aux Basques, Newfoundland & Labrador, and North Sydney, Nova Scotia to Argentia, Newfoundland & Labrador.

The Port aux Basques route is more frequently serviced, with multiple sailings per day, while the Argentia route operates less frequently, with sailings several times a week.

It's important to note that the journey times can vary based on weather conditions, so it's always a good idea to check the schedule and plan for potential delays.

The Bay Ferries service operates seasonally and offers one route: North Sydney, Nova Scotia to Port aux Basques, Newfoundland & Labrador. During peak season, there are multiple sailings per day, while during shoulder season, there may be fewer sailings available.

It's important to book in advance and check the schedule to ensure availability and avoid any last-minute changes.

It's also worth noting that there are additional ferry services available from other locations, such as the ferry from Portland, Maine to Yarmouth, Nova Scotia, which can provide an alternative route to accessing Newfoundland & Labrador via ferry.

However, it's important to plan accordingly and factor in travel time to and from these alternate locations.

Marine Atlantic
Website: https://www.marineatlantic.ca/

Bay Ferries
Website: https://www.ferries.ca/

Portland-Yarmouth ferry (operated by Nova Star Cruises)
Website: https://novastarcruises.com/

It's important to note that schedules and fares can vary depending on the time of year and other factors, so it's always a good idea to check the official websites for the most up-to-date information.

Tips for booking ferry tickets

Book in advance: Ferry services to Newfoundland & Labrador can be popular, especially during peak travel seasons, so it's a good idea to book your tickets in advance to secure your preferred departure dates and times.

Many ferry services allow you to book online or by phone, so be sure to check the official websites or call the ferry operators directly to reserve your tickets.

Be flexible with your travel dates: If you're able to be flexible with your travel dates, you may be able to find better deals on ferry tickets. Some ferry services offer discounts for midweek departures or early/late season travel, so consider adjusting your travel plans accordingly.

Check for package deals: Some ferry services offer package deals that include accommodations, car rentals, and other travel services. These packages can often save you money compared to booking each service separately, so be sure to check the ferry operator's website or call them directly to inquire about package deals.

Join loyalty programs: Some ferry services offer loyalty programs that allow you to earn points or discounts on future travel. If you plan to travel to Newfoundland & Labrador by ferry more than once, it may be worth joining the loyalty program to save money on future trips.

Be prepared for delays: Weather conditions and other factors can sometimes cause delays or cancellations of ferry services to Newfoundland & Labrador.

Be sure to check the ferry operator's website or call them directly for the latest information on any potential delays or cancellations, and plan accordingly by allowing extra time for your travels.

By following these tips, you can help ensure that you get the best possible deal on ferry tickets to Newfoundland & Labrador and enjoy a smooth, stress-free journey to this beautiful province.

Notes:

_____

_____

_____

_____

_____

By Land

While Newfoundland & Labrador is an island province, there are still plenty of opportunities to explore it by land. From scenic drives to hiking trails and historic sites, there are many ways to experience the beauty and culture of this unique destination.

In this section, we'll cover some of the top ways to explore Newfoundland & Labrador by land, including road trips, public transportation, and guided tours.

Whether you prefer to explore on your own or with a knowledgeable guide, there's something for everyone when it comes to exploring this beautiful province by land.

Driving to Newfoundland & Labrador from other parts of Canada and the United States

Driving to Newfoundland & Labrador can be a great way to explore the province's scenic beauty and charming communities. However, because Newfoundland & Labrador is an island province, you'll need to take a ferry or drive through another province to reach it by road.

If you're coming from other parts of Canada, the most common route is to take the Trans-Canada Highway to either North Sydney, Nova Scotia or

Port aux Basques, Newfoundland & Labrador, and then take a ferry to the other side.

The drive from major Canadian cities like Toronto, Ottawa, and Montreal to North Sydney, Nova Scotia can take anywhere from 16 to 22 hours, depending on your starting point and driving speed.

From there, the ferry ride to Port aux Basques takes approximately 6 hours, and there are several sailings per day during the peak travel season.

If you're coming from the United States, you'll need to cross the border into Canada and then follow the Trans-Canada Highway to reach the ferry terminals in Nova Scotia or Newfoundland & Labrador.

The closest major U.S. city to North Sydney, Nova Scotia is Boston, Massachusetts, which is approximately an 18-hour drive away. From there, you can take the ferry to Port aux Basques and then drive to your destination in Newfoundland & Labrador.

It's important to note that driving in Newfoundland & Labrador can be different from driving in other parts of Canada or the United States.

The roads can be narrow and winding in some areas, and weather conditions like fog, rain, and snow can make driving more challenging. It's also important to check ferry schedules and book your tickets in advance to ensure you can get to your destination on time.

Despite these challenges, driving to Newfoundland & Labrador can be a rewarding and memorable experience, offering stunning scenery and the chance to explore the province's unique culture and history at your own pace.

Public transportation options within the province

While driving is the most common way to get around Newfoundland & Labrador, there are also several public transportation options available within the province. These include:

Bus: There are several bus companies operating within Newfoundland & Labrador, including DRL Coachlines, Labrador Motors Limited, and Newhook's Transportation. These companies provide regular bus service to many communities within the province, as well as connections to other provinces and cities.

Taxis and ride-sharing services: Taxis and ride-sharing services like Uber and Lyft are available in some larger cities and towns in Newfoundland & Labrador, including St. John's and Corner Brook.

Train: While there are no passenger trains operating within Newfoundland & Labrador, the Newfoundland Railway Museum in Corner Brook offers a glimpse into the province's railway history.

Ferry: In addition to the ferries that connect Newfoundland & Labrador with other provinces, there are also several ferry services operating within the province.

These include the Bell Island Ferry, the Fogo Island Ferry, and the St. Brendan's Ferry, among others.

It's important to note that public transportation options can be limited in some areas of Newfoundland & Labrador, particularly in more remote or rural communities.

Additionally, schedules and availability may be affected by weather conditions or other factors, so it's a good idea to plan ahead and confirm transportation options before you travel.

Bus Company Links

DRL Coachlines:
 https://drlgroup.com/coachlines/

Labrador Motors Limited:
http://www.labradormotors.com/bus-services/

Newhook's Transportation:
https://www.newhooks.com/bus-services/

Please note that this list is not exhaustive and there may be other bus companies operating within the province. It's always a good idea to do some research and compare schedules and fares to find the best option for your needs.

Taxi Company Links

City Wide Taxi: https://citywidetaxi.ca/
Newfound Cabs: https://www.newfoundcabs.ca/
Jiffy Cabs: https://www.jiffycabs.ca/
Uber: https://www.uber.com/ca/en/ride/
Lyft: https://www.lyft.com/rider/cities/st-johns-nl-ca

Please note that these services may not be available in all areas of the province, and availability may vary depending on the time of day or demand. It's always a good idea to confirm availability and prices before you travel.

Car rental companies and tips for renting a car in Newfoundland & Labrador

Car rental is a popular option for visitors to Newfoundland & Labrador who want the freedom to explore the province on their own schedule. Here is some information on car rental companies and tips for renting a car in the province:

Car Rental Companies

Budget: https://www.budget.ca/en/locations/ca/nl
Enterprise: https://www.enterprise.ca/en/car-rental/locations/ca/nl
National: https://www.nationalcar.ca/en/home
Avis: https://www.avis.ca/en/locations/ca/nl
Hertz: https://www.hertz.ca/p/rental-car/canada/newfoundland

Tips for Renting a Car in Newfoundland & Labrador

Book in advance: Car rentals in Newfoundland & Labrador can be limited, especially during peak season, so it's a good idea to book your rental car well in advance.

Read the fine print: Make sure you understand the rental agreement, including any fees or restrictions that may apply.

Choose the right vehicle: Consider the size of your group and the type of driving you'll be doing. If you plan to drive on dirt or gravel roads, for example, a four-wheel-drive vehicle may be necessary.

Plan your route: Newfoundland & Labrador is a large province, and driving times can be longer than expected. Make sure you have a realistic plan for your trip and allow plenty of time for unexpected delays or stops.

Bring a GPS or map: Some areas of Newfoundland & Labrador have limited cell service, so it's a good idea to bring a GPS or paper map to help navigate.

It's also important to note that driving in Newfoundland & Labrador can be challenging, especially for those not accustomed to narrow, winding roads and varying weather conditions. It's always a good idea to drive cautiously and obey all traffic laws.

Overall, renting a car can be a great way to explore Newfoundland & Labrador on your own terms. Just be sure to plan ahead and choose a reputable rental company to ensure a safe and enjoyable trip.

Notes:

_____

_____

_____

_____

_____

_____

_____

_____

Practical Considerations

As with any travel destination, there are a number of practical considerations to keep in mind when planning a trip to Newfoundland & Labrador. In this section, we'll cover some important information about currency, language, safety, and more to help you prepare for your visit.

Weather and climate considerations

Weather and climate are important considerations when planning a trip to Newfoundland & Labrador, as the province experiences a wide range of weather conditions throughout the year. Here is some information on what to expect in terms of weather and climate, as well as some useful links for staying up-to-date on current conditions:

Climate: Newfoundland & Labrador has a subarctic climate, with long, cold winters and short, cool summers. Temperatures can vary widely depending on location and time of year, so it's important to check the forecast before you go.

Weather conditions: Newfoundland & Labrador is known for its rugged coastline, which can make for challenging driving conditions in the winter months.

Snow, ice, and high winds are common during the winter, while summer weather can be unpredictable, with fog, rain, and cool temperatures.

Useful links: To stay up-to-date on weather conditions in Newfoundland & Labrador, check out the following links:

Environment Canada
https://weather.gc.ca/canada_e.html

The Weather Network
https://www.theweathernetwork.com/ca/weather/newfoundland-and-labrador

Newfoundland & Labrador Tourism
https://www.newfoundlandlabrador.com/trip-ideas/travel-information/weather

When planning your trip to Newfoundland & Labrador, it's a good idea to pack for a variety of weather conditions and be prepared for unexpected changes in weather. Bring warm clothing, rain gear, and sturdy footwear to ensure a comfortable and enjoyable trip.

Passport and visa requirements

If you are planning a trip to Newfoundland & Labrador from outside of Canada, it's important to check the passport and visa requirements for your country. Here is some information on what you need to know.

Passport requirements: Visitors to Canada must have a valid passport or travel document that will be valid for the duration of their stay. Some countries may also require additional travel documents or visas, so it's important to check the requirements for your specific country.

Visa requirements: Depending on your country of origin, you may need a visa to enter Canada. The Government of Canada has a helpful tool called the "Electronic Travel Authorization" (eTA) that can be used to determine if you need a visa or other travel documents.

This tool can be accessed here:
https://www.canada.ca/en/immigration-refugees-citizenship/services/visit-canada/eta.html
Useful links: For more information on passport and visa requirements for visiting Canada and Newfoundland & Labrador, check out the following link.

Government of Canada:
https://www.canada.ca/en/immigration-refugees-citizenship/services/visit-canada.html

It's important to ensure that you have all the necessary travel documents before you arrive in Newfoundland & Labrador, as failure to do so can result in delays or denial of entry.

Customs and immigration procedures

If you are traveling to Newfoundland & Labrador from another country, you will need to go through customs and immigration procedures upon arrival in Canada.

Here are some important things to know:

Declarations: All travelers must complete a customs declaration form when entering Canada. This form asks about the items you are bringing into the country, including any goods or food. It is important to be honest and accurate when filling out this form, as false declarations can result in penalties.

Passport control: Upon arrival, you will go through passport control. You will need to present your passport or travel documents, as well as any visas or other required travel documents.

Border services: After passport control, you will proceed to the border services area. Here, your luggage will be inspected and you may be asked additional questions about your travel plans and the items you are bringing into the country.

Health and safety tips

When traveling to Newfoundland & Labrador, it's important to take health and safety precautions to protect yourself and others. Here are some important tips to keep in mind.

Vaccinations: Make sure you are up to date on routine vaccinations, such as measles-mumps-rubella (MMR) and seasonal flu.

Depending on your travel plans and medical history, you may also need additional vaccinations, such as hepatitis A or B, typhoid, or rabies. Consult with your doctor or a travel health clinic to determine what vaccinations are recommended for your trip.

Travel insurance: Consider purchasing travel insurance to protect yourself in case of unexpected medical emergencies, trip cancellations or interruptions, or lost or stolen belongings. Make sure you understand the terms and coverage of your policy before purchasing.

Safety tips: Newfoundland & Labrador is a generally safe destination, but it's always important to be aware of your surroundings and take basic safety precautions. For example, don't leave valuables unattended, stay in well-lit areas at night, and avoid walking alone in unfamiliar or isolated areas.

Weather and natural hazards: Newfoundland & Labrador can experience extreme weather conditions, such as snowstorms, heavy rain, and strong winds.

Make sure to check the weather forecast before you go and be prepared for changing conditions. Additionally, the province has many natural hazards, such as cliffs, rugged terrain, and potentially dangerous wildlife.

Follow posted signs and guidelines when exploring natural areas, and be cautious and respectful around wildlife.

Useful links: For more information on health and safety tips when traveling to Newfoundland & Labrador, check out the following links.

- Government of Canada travel health information: https://travel.gc.ca/travelling/health-safety

By taking the necessary health and safety precautions when traveling to Newfoundland & Labrador, you can help ensure a safe and enjoyable trip.

Notes:
_____
_____
_____
_____
_____
_____
_____
_____

Planning Your Trip

Now that you have a better understanding of the logistics involved in traveling to Newfoundland & Labrador, it's time to start planning your trip. In this section, we'll provide you with some helpful tips and resources for planning a memorable and enjoyable trip to this beautiful province.

Whether you're interested in outdoor adventures, cultural experiences, or simply relaxing and taking in the stunning scenery, Newfoundland & Labrador has something to offer every traveler. **So let's get started!**

Peak Season

The peak season in Newfoundland & Labrador is generally considered to be from late June to early September. During this time, the weather is generally warm and sunny, and many attractions and activities are in full swing.

This is the ideal time to explore the province's rugged coastline, hike its scenic trails, go whale watching, and experience the vibrant culture and history of its towns and cities.

One of the major benefits of visiting during the peak season is that you'll have access to the widest range of attractions and activities. Many businesses and tourist sites operate on seasonal schedules and may be closed during the off-season.

Additionally, the warmer weather and longer daylight hours make it easier to enjoy outdoor activities.

However, there are also some challenges to traveling during the peak season. First and foremost, it's a busy time of year, which means that accommodations, transportation, and popular tourist sites can be crowded and booked up far in advance. You may also encounter higher prices for flights, hotels, and activities during this time.

It's important to plan ahead if you're traveling during the peak season, and to be prepared for crowds and potentially higher costs.

But for many travelers, the benefits of visiting during this time outweigh the challenges, and the chance to experience Newfoundland & Labrador at its liveliest and most vibrant is well worth it.

The best time to visit Newfoundland & Labrador can vary depending on your interests and preferred activities.

Here are some general guidelines for the best times to visit for outdoor activities, festivals/events, and popular attractions:

Outdoor activities: The summer months of June through August are generally the best time to visit for outdoor activities such as hiking, camping, kayaking, and whale watching.

During this time, the weather is warm and pleasant, and the days are long with plenty of daylight to enjoy outdoor adventures.

Festivals and events: Newfoundland & Labrador is known for its lively festivals and events, many of which take place during the summer months.

Some of the most popular festivals include the George Street Festival in St. John's, the Newfoundland and Labrador Folk Festival in St. John's, and the Gros Morne Theatre Festival in Western Newfoundland.

Fall is also a great time to visit for events such as the Newfoundland and Labrador Craft Council's Christmas Craft Fair.

Popular attractions: Many of Newfoundland & Labrador's most popular attractions, such as Gros Morne National Park and L'Anse aux Meadows National Historic Site, are open from mid-May to mid-October.

Visiting during the shoulder seasons of May to June and September to October can be a great way to avoid crowds while still experiencing these must-see sights.

Overall, the best time to visit Newfoundland & Labrador depends on your individual interests and priorities. Whether you're looking to explore the outdoors, immerse yourself in local culture, or discover the province's history and heritage, there's a time of year that's perfect for you.

Shoulder Season

After the peak season, Newfoundland & Labrador enters the shoulder season, which is a time when the crowds have dispersed, the weather is mild, and the scenery is breathtaking.

The shoulder season, which typically runs from mid-August to mid-October, is an excellent time to visit the province, as the fall colors start to appear, and the hiking trails and parks are less crowded.

In this section, we will explore what to expect during the shoulder season and how to plan your trip accordingly.

The shoulder season in Newfoundland & Labrador falls between the peak season and the off-season, usually between mid-August to mid-October. During this time, the weather is cooler, and the summer crowds have dispersed, making it an ideal time to visit the province for those seeking a more relaxed and laid-back atmosphere.

One of the main benefits of visiting during the shoulder season is the beautiful fall foliage that blankets the province's forests and mountains, creating a breathtaking sight for visitors.

Additionally, many of the popular outdoor activities such as hiking, fishing, and wildlife viewing are still available, but with fewer crowds and a more tranquil setting.

One of the challenges of visiting during the shoulder season is the cooler weather, which can be unpredictable, with the possibility of rainfall and occasional fog.

As a result, visitors need to pack appropriately with warm clothing and rain gear to enjoy the outdoor activities fully. Additionally, some attractions and accommodations may have reduced operating hours or be closed during this period, so it's crucial to check ahead and plan accordingly.

Overall, the shoulder season in Newfoundland & Labrador offers a unique and less crowded travel experience, with beautiful fall foliage, cooler temperatures, and a relaxed atmosphere.

You can find more information about visiting Newfoundland & Labrador during shoulder season on the official tourism website.

https://www.newfoundlandlabrador.com/

Off-Season

If you're looking for a truly unique experience in Newfoundland & Labrador, consider visiting during the off-season.

While the weather may be colder and some attractions may be closed, the off-season offers a quieter and more authentic look at life in this beautiful province.

In this section, we'll explore the benefits and challenges of visiting during the off-season, as well as the best times to plan your trip.

The off-season in Newfoundland & Labrador typically runs from late fall to early spring. During this time, the weather can be chilly and some attractions and businesses may close for the season. However, there are many benefits to visiting during the off-season.

One major benefit is that you'll experience fewer crowds and more solitude. You can take in the stunning natural beauty of the province without having to compete with crowds of tourists.

In addition, many accommodations and activities offer reduced rates during the off-season, making it a more budget-friendly time to visit.

However, it's important to keep in mind that the weather during the off-season can be quite unpredictable and harsh. It's important to dress warmly and be prepared for snow, ice, and cold temperatures. Some roads and hiking trails may also be closed due to weather conditions.

The off-season in Newfoundland & Labrador typically runs from late fall to early spring, with some exceptions depending on the region.

During this time, the weather can be harsh with colder temperatures and occasional snowstorms. However, this time also has its benefits, including lower travel costs, fewer crowds, and unique experiences like winter sports and Northern Lights viewing.

Many winter festivals and events take place during this time, including the St. John's Ice Caps Hockey games and the Snow West Fest in Western Newfoundland.

Additionally, the off-season is a great time to visit for budget travelers, as accommodations and activities are often discounted.

Choosing Your Itinerary

When planning a trip to Newfoundland & Labrador, one of the most important decisions you'll make is choosing your itinerary. With so much to see and do in this beautiful province, it can be difficult to narrow down your options and decide where to go and what to see.

In this section, we'll provide some tips and suggestions to help you choose an itinerary that's right for you, based on your interests, travel style, and available time.

We'll also provide some resources to help you plan your itinerary and make the most of your time in Newfoundland & Labrador.

Regions of Newfoundland & Labrador

Newfoundland and Labrador is divided into several regions, each with its own unique geography, culture, and attractions. The main regions are Eastern, Central, Western, and Labrador.

The Eastern region of the province is known for its rugged coastline, picturesque fishing villages, and historic lighthouses. Visitors can explore the charming city of St. John's, hike the scenic East Coast Trail, and see icebergs and whales up close.

Central Newfoundland is a vast region of forests, rivers, and lakes, dotted with quaint towns and villages. Visitors can explore the Grand Falls-Windsor region, visit the Twillingate Islands, and hike the scenic coastal trails.

The Western region of the province is characterized by its stunning landscapes, including Gros Morne National Park, which is a UNESCO World Heritage Site. Visitors can explore the quaint fishing villages along the coast, take a boat tour of the fjords, and hike the rugged mountains and coastal trails.

Labrador is a remote and sparsely populated region of the province, known for its pristine wilderness, wildlife, and cultural heritage. Visitors can explore the rugged landscapes of Torngat Mountains National Park, learn about Labrador's Indigenous culture, and go fishing and hunting in the wilds.

Each region offers its own unique experiences and attractions, making it important to choose an itinerary that suits your interests and travel style.

1. Eastern Region: The Eastern region is home to the capital city of St. John's, which is known for its colorful houses, lively nightlife, and historical landmarks like Signal Hill and Cape Spear. This region is also home to the picturesque towns of Trinity and Bonavista, which offer a glimpse into Newfoundland's fishing and shipbuilding heritage.
2. Central Region: The Central region is known for its rugged landscapes, including the Long Range Mountains and Gros Morne National Park, which is a UNESCO World Heritage Site. Visitors can explore the fjords and hike the trails of the park, as well as take a boat tour to see icebergs and whales in the nearby waters.

3. Western Region: The Western region is the place to go for outdoor adventure, with opportunities for hiking, kayaking, and fishing. This region is also home to the Viking Trail, which follows the path of the Norse explorers who settled in Newfoundland over 1,000 years ago. Visitors can see Viking artifacts and learn about Norse history at the L'Anse aux Meadows National Historic Site.
4. Labrador: Labrador is a vast, sparsely populated region that offers unparalleled opportunities for wildlife viewing, including caribou, black bears, and bald eagles. Visitors can also explore the rugged coastlines and pristine forests, as well as learn about the indigenous Innu and Inuit cultures that have called Labrador home for thousands of years.

Each region of Newfoundland & Labrador offers a unique experience, and visitors are encouraged to explore them all to get a complete picture of the province's rich history and natural beauty.

Must-See Attractions

If you're planning a trip to Newfoundland & Labrador, you'll want to make sure you don't miss out on some of the province's must-see attractions. From stunning natural scenery to rich cultural experiences, there is no shortage of things to see and do in this beautiful part of Canada.
In this section, we'll highlight some of the top attractions that should be on every visitor's itinerary. Whether you're interested in outdoor adventures, historical sites, or cultural events, there's something for everyone in Newfoundland & Labrador.

1. Gros Morne National Park - a UNESCO World Heritage Site with stunning fjords, mountains, and hiking trails.
2. L'Anse aux Meadows National Historic Site - a Viking settlement dating back to the 11th century.
3. Signal Hill National Historic Site - a historic site with panoramic views of St. John's Harbour and the Atlantic Ocean.
4. The Rooms - a cultural center with exhibits and galleries showcasing the history and culture of Newfoundland & Labrador.
5. Cape Spear Lighthouse National Historic Site - the easternmost point in North America with stunning views of the Atlantic Ocean.

6. Fogo Island - a unique island community with a rich cultural heritage and stunning natural scenery.
7. Terra Nova National Park - a beautiful park with hiking trails, campgrounds, and stunning coastline views.
8. Red Bay National Historic Site - a UNESCO World Heritage Site with a fascinating history of whaling and Basque culture.
9. Quidi Vidi Village - a picturesque fishing village in St. John's with a brewery, art galleries, and hiking trails.
10. The Viking Trail - a scenic drive through the stunning landscapes of western Newfoundland, passing by fjords, waterfalls, and wildlife.

These are just a few of the many must-see attractions in Newfoundland & Labrador that showcase the province's natural beauty, rich history, and vibrant culture.

1. **Gros Morne National Park** - Located on the west coast of Newfoundland, Gros Morne National Park is a UNESCO World Heritage Site and one of the most stunning natural areas in Canada. The park is home to a unique geological landscape, including the Tablelands, a mountain range made up of peridotite, a rare type of rock not found anywhere else in the world. Visitors can

enjoy hiking, camping, kayaking, and wildlife watching in this beautiful park.

2. **L'Anse aux Meadows National Historic Site** - This site on the northern tip of Newfoundland is the only known Viking settlement in North America, dating back to the 11th century. Visitors can tour reconstructed Viking buildings, learn about Norse history and culture, and explore the surrounding landscape, including the nearby UNESCO World Heritage Site of Red Bay, a Basque whaling station.

3. **Signal Hill National Historic Site** - Located in St. John's, Signal Hill is a historic landmark that played a crucial role in the defense of the city during various wars. Visitors can hike to the top of the hill for stunning views of the city and the ocean, and explore the many historical sites, including Cabot Tower and the remains of fortifications.

4. **The Rooms** - The Rooms is a cultural center in St. John's that houses a museum, art gallery, and archives, showcasing the history, art, and culture of Newfoundland and Labrador. Visitors can learn about the province's Aboriginal, Viking, and European roots, as well as its contemporary art scene.

5. **Cape Spear Lighthouse National Historic Site** - Located just outside St. John's, Cape

Spear is the easternmost point in North America and home to a historic lighthouse that has been guiding ships for over 150 years. Visitors can explore the lighthouse and enjoy breathtaking views of the Atlantic Ocean.

6. **Twillingate** - This small town on the northeastern coast of Newfoundland is known as the "Iceberg Capital of the World" and is a popular destination for whale watching and iceberg spotting. Visitors can also enjoy hiking, kayaking, and exploring the charming fishing villages in the area.

7. **Fogo Island** - Located off the northeastern coast of Newfoundland, Fogo Island is a remote and stunningly beautiful destination known for its unique culture and modern architecture. Visitors can stay in one of the island's famous "fishing shacks" or luxury resorts, and enjoy hiking, kayaking, and cultural experiences.

8. **Terra Nova National Park** - Located on the east coast of Newfoundland, Terra Nova National Park is a popular destination for outdoor activities such as camping, hiking, and boating. Visitors can explore the park's many lakes, rivers, and forests, as well as learn about the history and culture of the region.

9. **The Viking Trail** - The Viking Trail is a scenic drive along the northern coast of Newfoundland, taking visitors through picturesque fishing villages, historic sites, and stunning natural landscapes. Highlights include L'Anse aux Meadows, Gros Morne National Park, and the many lighthouses and whale watching spots along the way.

10. **Torngat Mountains National Park** - Located in northern Labrador, Torngat Mountains National Park is a remote and rugged wilderness area known for its stunning landscapes and unique wildlife, including polar bears and caribou. Visitors can enjoy hiking, kayaking, and cultural experiences with the Inuit people who call the region home.

https://www.newfoundlandlabrador.com/top-destinations

Accommodations

In this section, we will discuss accommodation options available throughout the province.

Whether you are looking for a luxury hotel, cozy bed and breakfast, or a campsite under the stars, Newfoundland & Labrador has a range of options to suit any traveler's needs and preferences.

From charming seaside inns to rugged wilderness lodges, there is no shortage of unique and comfortable places to stay in this beautiful part of Canada. So let's dive in and explore the many accommodation options available in Newfoundland & Labrador.

Types of Accommodations

Newfoundland & Labrador offers a diverse range of accommodations to suit all tastes and budgets. Visitors can choose from luxurious hotels and resorts to charming bed and breakfasts, cozy vacation rentals, and rustic campgrounds. Whether you're planning a romantic getaway, a family vacation, or a solo adventure, there's a perfect place to stay in this beautiful province.

1. Hotels: Hotels offer a range of amenities and services, from basic to luxurious. They are usually located in urban or tourist areas, making them convenient for exploring the local attractions. However, they can be more expensive than other types of accommodation.

2. Bed and Breakfasts: Bed and Breakfasts provide a more intimate and personalized experience than hotels. They are often located in historic or scenic areas, and offer home-cooked meals and local knowledge.

However, they may have limited amenities and services.

3. Vacation Rentals: Vacation rentals offer the comforts of home, such as a kitchen and living space, and can be a good option for families or groups. They are often located in rural or remote areas, providing a peaceful and secluded experience. However, they may require a longer drive to reach popular tourist destinations.

4. Campgrounds: Campgrounds provide a budget-friendly and outdoor experience. They are often located in scenic areas, such as national parks, and offer a range of activities, such as hiking and fishing. However, they may not offer the same level of comfort and convenience as other types of accommodation.

It's important to choose the type of accommodation that best suits your needs and preferences, taking into consideration factors such as location, price, and amenities.

- https://www.newfoundlandlabrador.com/plan-and-book/accommodations
- https://www.newfoundlandlabrador.com/things-to-do/camping

Booking Your Accommodations

If you're planning a trip to Newfoundland & Labrador, here are some tips for booking accommodations:

1. **Book early:** During peak season, accommodations can fill up quickly, so it's best to book as early as possible to ensure you get the type of accommodations you want.
2. Use booking websites: Websites like Booking.com, Expedia, and Airbnb can help you find a wide range of accommodations at different price points.
3. Consider location: Think about what areas you want to visit and choose accommodations that are conveniently located.
4. Read reviews: Before booking any accommodations, read reviews from other travelers to get an idea of the quality of the accommodations and the experience other travelers had.
5. Look for deals: Check for any deals or promotions offered by accommodations, such as discounts for booking in advance or for longer stays.
6. Contact accommodations directly: If you have specific needs or requests, it may be helpful to contact accommodations directly to ensure they can accommodate you.

Here are some links to help you find accommodations in Newfoundland & Labrador:
- Newfoundland & Labrador Tourism Accommodations: https://www.newfoundlandlabrador.com/plan-and-book/accommodations
- Airbnb Newfoundland & Labrador: https://www.airbnb.ca/s/Newfoundland-and-Labrador--Canada/homes?refinement_paths%5B%5D=%2Fhomes&place_id=ChIJqwS6WKeY_ksRgWLEcTaZv4c&search_type=UNKNOWN&adults=1

Activities and Tours

Activities and Tours are an essential part of planning your trip to Newfoundland & Labrador, as they offer a chance to experience the unique culture, scenery, and wildlife of the province. From hiking to kayaking, whale watching to iceberg tours, there are many options for visitors to choose from.

In this section, we will provide an overview of the different types of activities and tours available in Newfoundland & Labrador, as well as tips for choosing the best options for your trip. We will also include links to helpful resources to help you plan your activities and tours.

Outdoor Activities

Newfoundland & Labrador is a haven for outdoor enthusiasts, offering a wide range of activities to suit every interest and skill level.

Whether you're looking to explore the rugged coastline, hike through pristine wilderness, or spot majestic wildlife, there are plenty of options to choose from.

Some of the top activities to do in Newfoundland & Labrador include hiking, fishing, kayaking, and wildlife watching, as well as cultural experiences like attending local festivals and events. With so much to see and do, it's important to plan your activities and tours in advance to make the most of your trip.

1. Hiking: Newfoundland & Labrador has an abundance of hiking trails that range from easy strolls to challenging treks. Some of the most popular trails include the East Coast Trail, Gros Morne National Park, and the Long Range Traverse.
2. Fishing: Newfoundland & Labrador is known for its excellent fishing opportunities, especially for Atlantic salmon and trout. Some of the top fishing destinations include the Humber River, the Exploits River, and the Labrador coast.
3. Kayaking: With its rugged coastline and abundant marine life, Newfoundland &

Labrador is a paradise for kayakers. Some of the top places to paddle include Gros Morne National Park, Trinity Bay, and the Bay of Islands.
4. Wildlife watching: Newfoundland & Labrador is home to a variety of wildlife, including moose, caribou, whales, and seabirds. Some of the best places to see wildlife include Terra Nova National Park, Cape St. Mary's Ecological Reserve, and the Witless Bay Ecological Reserve.

Permits and gear requirements vary depending on the activity and location, so it's important to do your research before heading out.

https://www.newfoundlandlabrador.com/things-to-do/hiking-and-walking

https://www.newfoundlandlabrador.com/things-to-do/kayaking-rafting-and-diving

https://www.newfoundlandlabrador.com/things-to-do/birdwatching

Cultural Activities

Newfoundland & Labrador is rich in culture and history, and there are many cultural activities to experience while visiting the province.

Some of the top cultural activities include attending one of the many festivals and events that take place throughout the year, visiting museums and art galleries, exploring historical sites, and learning about Indigenous culture and traditions.

Newfoundland & Labrador is home to a vibrant arts scene, and there are many festivals and events that celebrate the province's cultural heritage. One of the most popular events is the George Street Festival, a week-long music festival that takes place in downtown St. John's every August. Other popular events include the Gros Morne Theatre Festival, the Newfoundland and Labrador Folk Festival, and the East Coast Music Awards.

The province is also home to a number of museums and art galleries, where visitors can learn about the province's history and culture. The Rooms in St. John's is a must-visit, with exhibits covering everything from the province's natural history to its art and music. Other notable museums include the Johnson Geo Centre, the Ryan Premises National Historic Site, and the Labrador Interpretation Center.

In addition to these cultural activities, visitors to Newfoundland & Labrador can also learn about **Indigenous culture and traditions**. The province is home to the Innu, Inuit, and Mi'kmaq peoples, and there are many opportunities to learn about their cultures and histories.

The Quidi Vidi Village Plantation in St. John's is a great place to start, with exhibits and workshops showcasing Indigenous arts and crafts. Visitors can also take guided tours of Indigenous communities and learn about traditional hunting and fishing practices.

Links to Newfoundland & Labrador Tourism website with more information on cultural activities:

1. Attend a Festival: Newfoundland & Labrador is known for its vibrant and unique festivals that celebrate everything from music to food. Some of the top festivals include the George Street Festival in St. John's, the Writers at Woody Point Festival on the west coast, and the Fish, Fun, and Folk Festival in Twillingate.

https://www.newfoundlandlabrador.com/things-to-do/festivals-and-events

2. Visit Museums: The province is home to many museums that showcase its rich history and culture. Some must-visit museums include The Rooms in St. John's, which houses exhibits on the province's natural and cultural history, and the Grenfell Interpretation Centre in St. Anthony, which highlights the work of Sir Wilfred Grenfell and the history of the area.

https://www.newfoundlandlabrador.com/things-to-do/museums-and-historic-sites

3. Learn about Indigenous Culture: Newfoundland & Labrador is also home to several Indigenous communities, including the Innu and Mi'kmaq. Visitors can learn about the history and culture of these communities through cultural tours and experiences, such as the Tea and Tradition Tour in Miawpukek First Nation.

Links to Newfoundland & Labrador Tourism website with more information on each activity:

Guided Tours

Newfoundland & Labrador offers a variety of guided tour options to suit different interests and preferences.

Group tours are a popular option for visitors who want to join a pre-planned itinerary and travel with a group of like-minded individuals. Private tours offer more flexibility and personalization, allowing visitors to customize their itinerary and travel at their own pace.

Self-guided tours are another option for independent travelers who prefer to explore on their own, with the assistance of pre-planned routes and recommendations.

Guided tours in Newfoundland & Labrador cover a range of activities and themes, including hiking, wildlife watching, cultural tours, and historical tours. Many tour operators also offer packages that combine multiple activities and experiences, such as a hiking and whale watching tour or a cultural and culinary tour.

Whether you prefer to join a group tour or create your own itinerary, guided tours can be a great way to experience the best of Newfoundland & Labrador and gain a deeper understanding of the region's culture and history.

Group Tours:
1. Group tours are typically led by a tour guide and include a set itinerary for a specific group of people. The benefits of a group tour include the opportunity to meet new people, the convenience of having a planned itinerary, and often lower costs due to the group discount. However, the drawbacks may include less flexibility in the itinerary and less personalized attention from the guide.

Private Tours:
2. Private tours are more customizable and can be tailored to the specific interests of the individual or group. The benefits of a

private tour include more flexibility in the itinerary, the ability to ask questions and interact with the guide more easily, and a more personalized experience. However, private tours can be more expensive than group tours, and may not offer the same discounts for large groups.

Self-Guided Tours:
3. Self-guided tours provide the most flexibility in terms of itinerary and scheduling. The benefits of a self-guided tour include the ability to explore at your own pace, the opportunity to deviate from the planned route, and potentially lower costs. However, self-guided tours require more planning and research, and may not provide the same level of expertise and insight as a guided tour.

- Wildland Tours: https://wildlands.com/
- Linkum Tours: https://linkumtours.com/
- CapeRace Cultural Adventures: https://caperace.com/

Dining and Cuisine

Newfoundland and Labrador is a culinary destination that offers unique and delicious food experiences.

From fresh seafood to wild game, the region's cuisine reflects its history, geography, and diverse cultural influences. In this section, we'll explore the best places to eat in Newfoundland and Labrador, as well as the must-try local dishes and drinks.

Whether you're looking for a fine dining experience or a casual meal, there's something for every taste and budget in this province.

Regional Cuisine

Newfoundland & Labrador is known for its unique and delicious cuisine that reflects its history, culture, and natural resources.

With an abundance of fresh seafood, wild game, and local produce, the region has developed a distinct culinary identity that draws inspiration from both traditional and modern cooking techniques.

From hearty stews to freshly caught fish, Newfoundland & Labrador's cuisine is a must-try for any food lover.

One of the most iconic dishes in Newfoundland & Labrador is Jiggs Dinner, which is a traditional Sunday roast made with salt beef, root vegetables, and peas pudding. Another popular dish is cod tongues, which are deep-fried and served with scrunchions (bits of fried salt pork).
Seafood chowder, fish and chips, and lobster are also local favorites.

In addition to its traditional dishes, Newfoundland & Labrador also has a growing craft beer scene and a thriving culinary tourism industry, with many restaurants and food tours showcasing the region's unique ingredients and flavors.

Whether you're a foodie or just looking to try something new, Newfoundland & Labrador's cuisine is sure to leave a lasting impression.

Some of the best places to try regional cuisine in Newfoundland & Labrador include:

1. **Raymonds Restaurant** in St. John's - known for its modern take on traditional Newfoundland dishes and its focus on locally sourced ingredients.
2. **The Merchant Tavern** in St. John's - offers a seasonal menu of contemporary Newfoundland cuisine with a focus on seafood.
3. **The Fish Exchange** in St. John's - a seafood market and restaurant where you can sample fresh fish and shellfish cooked to order.
4. **The Norseman** Restaurant and Gaia Art Gallery in L'Anse aux Meadows - serves traditional Newfoundland dishes and has a gallery featuring local artists.
5. **The Bonavista Social Club** in Bonavista - specializes in wood-fired sourdough pizza and other dishes made with locally sourced ingredients.

Exploring St. John's

Welcome to St. John's, the vibrant capital city of Newfoundland & Labrador! This historic city is known for its colorful row houses, lively downtown area, and stunning natural surroundings.

Whether you're looking to explore the city's rich history, enjoy local cuisine, or take in the beautiful scenery, there's something for everyone in St. John's. In this section, we'll cover some of the top things to do and see in St. John's, as well as some helpful tips for planning your visit.

History of the city

St. John's is the capital city of Newfoundland & Labrador and has a rich history that dates back to the 16th century. The city was originally a fishing village for the Basque and Portuguese, but it was officially founded in 1583 by Sir Humphrey Gilbert, an English explorer.

Throughout the centuries, St. John's has played a significant role in the history of North America, serving as a strategic military base during both World War I and World War II. Today, the city is a vibrant cultural hub and one of the oldest European settlements in North America.

Top things to do and see

St. John's, the capital city of Newfoundland & Labrador, is a vibrant and historic city with plenty to see and do. Here are some top things to do and see:

1. **Signal Hill:** This National Historic Site is a must-visit for its stunning views of the city, the Atlantic Ocean, and its connection to Canadian history, including its role in the famous Battle of Signal Hill.
2. **The Rooms**: This museum and cultural center showcases the art, history, and culture of Newfoundland & Labrador, with exhibits on everything from the Titanic disaster to local folk music.
3. **Quidi Vidi Village**: This picturesque fishing village within the city limits is a great place to explore historic houses, art studios, and craft breweries.
4. **George Street**: This pedestrian-only street is known for its lively nightlife, with pubs, bars, and live music venues lining the street.
5. **Cape Spear Lighthouse**: Located just outside the city, Cape Spear is the easternmost point of North America and offers spectacular ocean views and the chance to spot whales and other wildlife.
6. **Petty Harbour:** This charming fishing village just a short drive from St. John's offers stunning coastal views, walking trails, and the chance to go whale watching or fishing.

7. **Johnson Geo Centre**: This interactive geological museum offers exhibits on the earth's history and the unique geology of Newfoundland & Labrador, as well as a 3D theater and hiking trails.
8. **St. John's Farmers' Market**: Held on Saturdays, this popular farmers' market offers a chance to sample local food, crafts, and music.
9. **Bannerman Park**: This historic park in the heart of the city offers walking trails, playgrounds, and the chance to relax in a beautiful green space.
10. **St. John's Haunted Hike**: For those interested in the paranormal, this guided walking tour explores the city's ghost stories and legends.

Where to eat, drink, and shop

St. John's has a vibrant culinary scene with a range of options to suit all tastes and budgets. For a taste of local cuisine, visitors can try traditional Newfoundland dishes such as cod tongues, fish and brews, and toutons at places like the Merchant Tavern, Mallard Cottage, and Raymonds.

There are also plenty of international options, including sushi at Basho, Indian cuisine at India Gate, and Italian fare at Piatto Pizzeria.
When it comes to drinks, St. John's has a lively nightlife with plenty of bars and pubs to choose from.

For a pint of locally brewed beer, visitors can head to Quidi Vidi Brewery or YellowBelly Brewery, both of which also offer tours and tastings. For a unique cocktail experience, The Fifth Ticket serves up creative drinks made with local ingredients.

Shoppers can find a range of locally made products and souvenirs at shops like Nonia, which specializes in hand-knit clothing and accessories, and the Newfoundland Chocolate Company, which offers a range of sweet treats made with local ingredients.

The downtown area also has a mix of boutiques and larger stores, including the historic Murray's Garden Centre and the boutique clothing shop Envy.

Insider tips from locals

- Take a hike up to Signal Hill at sunset to catch the stunning views over the city and harbor.
- Visit the Quidi Vidi Village to try local beer and see the picturesque fishing village.
- Check out the local food scene on Duckworth and Water Streets for some of the best seafood and pub fare in town.
- Explore the side streets and alleyways for hidden gems like art galleries and boutique shops.
- Take a walk along George Street to experience the nightlife and live music scene that St. John's is famous for.

Overall, locals recommend taking your time to explore the city on foot to really get a feel for the unique charm and character of St. John's.

The East Coast Trail

The East Coast Trail is a breathtaking 300-kilometer coastal walking and hiking trail that winds through stunning cliffs, sea stacks, fjords, and forests, offering unparalleled views of the rugged coastline of Newfoundland's Avalon Peninsula.

The trail stretches from Cape St. Francis to Cappahayden and offers a unique opportunity to explore the natural beauty and cultural heritage of the area, with access to historic sites, seabird colonies, whales, and icebergs along the way.

Whether you're a seasoned hiker or a casual walker, the East Coast Trail has something for everyone, making it a must-see attraction for any visitor to Newfoundland and Labrador.

Overview of the trail and its history

The East Coast Trail is a world-renowned coastal hiking trail that spans 336 kilometers (209 miles) along the eastern coast of the Avalon Peninsula in Newfoundland, Canada.

The trail is divided into 26 wilderness paths that take hikers through rugged coastline, dramatic cliffs, and picturesque fishing villages.

The East Coast Trail has a rich history, as it follows the same path used by Indigenous people and European settlers for thousands of years.

Today, the trail is a popular destination for hiking enthusiasts from all over the world, offering unparalleled views of the Atlantic Ocean and the opportunity to explore Newfoundland's natural beauty.

Recommendations for the best hikes

It offers hikers a chance to experience stunning views of the Atlantic Ocean, towering cliffs, and picturesque coves. With so many trails to choose from, it can be difficult to know where to start.

However, some of the most popular and rewarding hikes on the trail include the Spout Path, the North Head Trail, and the Sugarloaf Path. Each of these hikes offers a unique perspective on the natural beauty of Newfoundland's coastline and is sure to leave a lasting impression.

Safety tips and what to bring

When hiking on the East Coast Trail, it's important to prioritize safety. Here are some tips to ensure a safe and enjoyable hiking experience:
1. Check the weather forecast before you go and prepare accordingly. Bring layers of

clothing, including a waterproof jacket, hat, and gloves.
2. Bring enough water and food for your hike. It's recommended to bring at least 2 liters of water per person for a day hike.
3. Wear sturdy hiking shoes or boots with good ankle support.
4. Stay on marked trails and follow all signs and warnings.
5. Tell someone your hiking plans and expected return time.
6. Bring a fully charged cell phone, map, and compass.
7. Be aware of wildlife in the area, such as moose and black bears, and keep a safe distance.
8. Leave no trace and pack out all trash and litter.

By following these safety tips and preparing properly, you can have a safe and enjoyable hiking experience on the East Coast Trail.

Accommodation options along the trail

There are several accommodation options along the East Coast Trail, ranging from camping to bed and breakfasts. Some of the campsites along the trail include La Manche Provincial Park, Tinkers Point Pond, and Bauline East Municipal Park.

For those looking for a more comfortable stay, there are several bed and breakfasts along the trail, such as the Hares Ears Cottage in Petty Harbour and the

Captain's Quarters in Bay Bulls. It's important to note that booking ahead is necessary for most accommodation options, especially during peak hiking season.

East Coast Trail Association:
https://eastcoasttrail.com/

Notes:

Gros Morne National Park

Located on the west coast of Newfoundland, Gros Morne National Park is one of Canada's most beautiful and rugged national parks. It was designated a UNESCO World Heritage Site in 1987, thanks to its unique geology and diverse wildlife.

The park offers visitors a chance to explore fjords, mountains, and forests, and to learn about the region's rich history and culture. Whether you're an avid hiker, a wildlife enthusiast, or simply looking for a place to relax and unwind, Gros Morne has something for everyone.

In this section, we'll explore some of the top things to do and see in Gros Morne National Park, as well as where to stay and how to make the most of your visit.

Overview of the park and its history

Gros Morne National Park is a UNESCO World Heritage Site located on the west coast of Newfoundland, Canada.

The park encompasses over 1,800 square kilometers of rugged, mountainous terrain and is home to a diverse range of wildlife, including moose, caribou, and black bears.

The park's geology is also of significant scientific importance, featuring some of the world's best examples of plate tectonics and ancient rock formations.

With its stunning scenery and unique natural features, Gros Morne National Park is a must-see destination for visitors to Newfoundland and Labrador.

Top things to do and see

Gros Morne National Park is one of the most popular destinations in Newfoundland & Labrador, known for its stunning natural beauty and unique geological features.

Some of the top things to do and see in the park include hiking the Tablelands, a rare section of the earth's mantle exposed above ground, exploring the fjords of Western Brook Pond, and discovering the breathtaking Green Gardens.

With so much to see and do, Gros Morne National Park is a must-visit destination for nature lovers and outdoor enthusiasts alike.

Hiking and camping recommendations

There are many great hiking and camping options in Gros Morne National Park. Some of the top hikes in the park include the Tablelands Trail, Green Gardens Trail, and Gros Morne Mountain Trail.

Each of these hikes offers stunning views and unique terrain.

When it comes to camping, there are four campgrounds within the park: Berry Hill, Green Point, Lomond, and Shallow Bay. All of the campgrounds offer different amenities and locations within the park, so it's important to research which one will best suit your needs.

There are also backcountry camping options available in designated areas throughout the park, but permits are required and should be obtained in advance.

It's important to note that the weather in Gros Morne National Park can be unpredictable, so be prepared for all types of weather and pack accordingly. Additionally, be sure to follow Leave No Trace principles and properly dispose of all waste to preserve the natural beauty of the park.

Newfoundland & Labrador Tourism
https://www.newfoundlandlabrador.com/things-to-do/hiking-and-walking

Parks Canada - Gros Morne National Park - Hiking
https://www.pc.gc.ca/en/pn-np/nl/grosmorne/activ/randonnee-hiking

Parks Canada - Gros Morne National Park - Camping
https://www.pc.gc.ca/en/pn-np/nl/grosmorne/activ/camping

Wildlife and nature photography tips

Here are some wildlife and nature photography tips for visiting Gros Morne National Park:
1. Use a telephoto lens: Wildlife, such as moose and caribou, can be seen in the park. Using a telephoto lens will allow you to capture images of these animals from a distance, without disturbing them.
2. Be patient: Wildlife sightings can be unpredictable, so be prepared to wait for the perfect shot.
3. Golden Hour: The hour before sunrise and the hour after sunset (known as golden hour) is the best time to capture stunning natural landscapes.
4. Composition: Consider the composition of your image. Use the rule of thirds to create an interesting composition and lead the viewer's eye through the image.
5. Lighting: Lighting is key in photography. Try to shoot during the early morning or late afternoon when the light is soft and warm.
6. Tripod: Use a tripod to keep your camera steady and prevent any blurry images.
7. Research: Research the park and its wildlife before you go. This will help you know what to expect and plan your photography accordingly.

8. Respect wildlife: When photographing wildlife, always remember to respect their space and observe them from a distance to avoid causing any disturbance.
9. Experiment: Don't be afraid to experiment with different angles and settings to create unique and creative images.
10. Practice: The more you practice, the better you will become. Take advantage of the park's stunning landscapes and wildlife to practice your skills.

Notes:

_____

_____

_____

_____

_____

_____

_____

_____

Labrador

Located in the eastern part of Canada, Labrador is a region that covers more than 294,000 square kilometers, making up about 72% of the province of Newfoundland and Labrador.

It is known for its stunning natural beauty, rich cultural heritage, and unique wildlife. Labrador offers a wide range of activities and experiences for visitors, from hiking and fishing to learning about Indigenous culture and history.

In this section, we will provide an overview of the top things to do and see in Labrador, as well as some recommendations for accommodations and guided tours.

Overview of the region and its history

Labrador is the mainland portion of the province of Newfoundland and Labrador, located in eastern Canada. It is the easternmost part of the Canadian Shield and is known for its rugged and remote landscape, including vast stretches of wilderness, pristine lakes and rivers, and breathtaking coastal vistas.

The region has a rich history, with Indigenous peoples having lived there for thousands of years before the arrival of European explorers and settlers.

Today, Labrador is home to a mix of Indigenous communities, small towns, and mining and resource extraction industries, as well as a growing tourism industry focused on outdoor adventure and cultural experiences.

Top things to do and see

Some of the top things to do and see in Labrador include:
1. Torngat Mountains National Park: This park is known for its stunning fjords, glaciers, and mountain peaks. It's also home to a variety of wildlife, including polar bears, caribou, and eagles.
2. Red Bay National Historic Site: This site was once a major whaling station in the 16th century and is now a UNESCO World Heritage Site. Visitors can explore the ruins of the station and learn about the history of the whaling industry in Labrador.
3. Battle Harbour Historic Site: This restored fishing village was once one of the busiest ports in Labrador and is now a popular tourist destination. Visitors can tour the historic buildings, go fishing or hiking, and enjoy traditional Newfoundland and Labrador cuisine.
4. Churchill Falls: This hydroelectric power station is one of the largest in the world and is a marvel of modern engineering. Visitors can take a guided tour of the facility and learn about how it produces electricity.

5. Labrador Coastal Drive: This scenic drive takes visitors along the rugged coast of Labrador, passing through picturesque fishing villages, rocky beaches, and stunning natural landscapes.
6. Labrador Pioneer Footpath: This 65-km hiking trail runs from Pinware River Provincial Park to L'Anse-au-Clair and offers stunning views of the coast and surrounding wilderness.
7. Cultural experiences: Labrador is home to several Indigenous communities, including the Innu and Nunatsiavut people. Visitors can learn about their culture and traditions through guided tours, art exhibits, and cultural festivals.

These are just a few of the top things to do and see in Labrador. The region is known for its stunning natural beauty, rich history, and unique cultural experiences.

1. Torngat Mountains National Park: https://www.pc.gc.ca/en/pn-np/nl/torngats
2. Red Bay National Historic Site: https://www.pc.gc.ca/en/lhn-nhs/nl/redbay
3. Battle Harbour National Historic District: https://www.battleharbour.com/
4. Labrador Pioneer Footpath: https://www.labradorpioneerfootpath.com/
5. Lawrence O'Brien Arts Centre: http://www.obrienartscentre.ca/
6. Mealy Mountains National Park Reserve: https://www.pc.gc.ca/en/pn-np/nl/mealy

7. The Labrador Straits Museum: http://www.labradorstraitsmuseum.ca/

For more……

https://www.newfoundlandlabrador.com/search?q=places+to+stay

Travel tips and advice for visiting Labrador

Here are some travel tips and advice for visiting Labrador:
1. Plan your trip ahead of time: Labrador is a remote and vast region with limited infrastructure, so it's important to plan your trip ahead of time. Decide on the places you want to visit, how you will get there, and where you will stay.
2. Prepare for the weather: Labrador has a harsh and unpredictable climate, so it's important to be prepared for any weather conditions. Bring warm and waterproof clothing, especially if you plan to visit during the winter months.
3. Consider transportation options: Labrador is only accessible by air or sea. There are no roads connecting the region to the rest of Canada, so you'll need to fly or take a ferry. If you plan to explore the region, renting a car may be a good option.
4. Respect the local culture: Labrador has a rich Indigenous culture, and it's important to respect the local customs and traditions.

Learn about the Inuit and Innu culture and history before you visit, and be mindful of the cultural sensitivities.
5. Bring a camera: Labrador is a beautiful and remote region with stunning landscapes and wildlife. Don't forget to bring a camera to capture the memories.
6. Be mindful of wildlife: Labrador is home to a variety of wildlife, including polar bears, black bears, caribou, and moose. If you plan to hike or camp in the region, be mindful of the wildlife and follow safety guidelines.
7. Bring cash: Some parts of Labrador have limited or no access to banking services, so it's important to bring cash for any purchases or expenses.
8. Check for seasonal closures: Some attractions, accommodations, and services in Labrador may be closed during the off-season or due to weather conditions, so it's important to check for seasonal closures before you visit.
9. Plan for limited internet and cell service: Labrador is a remote region with limited internet and cell service, especially in more remote areas. Plan accordingly and be prepared to disconnect during your visit.
10. Pack a sense of adventure: Labrador is a remote and wild region with plenty of opportunities for adventure and exploration. Pack a sense of adventure and be open to new experiences.

Notes:

_____

_____

_____

Activities and Adventures

Newfoundland and Labrador are full of thrilling outdoor activities and adventures to keep visitors entertained and engaged.

From exploring stunning natural landscapes to experiencing unique cultural traditions, there is no shortage of things to do and see.

Whether you're seeking a heart-pumping adrenaline rush or a peaceful nature retreat, this province has something for everyone.

In this section, we'll cover some of the top activities and adventures available in Newfoundland and Labrador, along with recommendations for the best places to try them.

Whale watching

Newfoundland and Labrador is one of the best places in the world to go whale watching. With its location in the Atlantic Ocean, the region offers a unique opportunity to see a variety of whale species, including humpback, minke, and orca whales.

Whale watching is a popular activity for visitors, and there are many tour operators that offer guided tours for whale watching in Newfoundland and Labrador.

In this section, we will explore everything you need to know about whale watching in the region, including the best time to go, the best places to see whales, and how to book a whale watching tour.

- Gatherall's Puffin & Whale Watch - https://gatheralls.com/
- O'Brien's Whale & Bird Tours - https://obriensboattours.com/
- Iceberg Quest Ocean Tours - https://icebergquest.com/
- Sea of Whales Adventures - https://www.seaofwhales.com/
- BonTours - https://www.bontours.ca/
- Twillingate Adventure Tours - https://www.twillingateadventuretours.com/
- Trinity Eco-Tours - https://trinityecotours.com/
- Coastal Connections - https://coastalconnections.ca/

- Whale House Guest House - https://www.whalehouse.ca/
- Northland Discovery Boat Tours - https://www.discovernorthland.com/

Iceberg Spotting

Iceberg spotting is a popular activity in Newfoundland & Labrador, particularly in the spring and early summer months when icebergs are most commonly seen along the coast. Here are some links for iceberg spotting:

1. Iceberg Finder: This website provides real-time information on the location of icebergs in Newfoundland & Labrador, making it a great resource for planning your iceberg spotting adventure.
   https://www.icebergfinder.com/

2. Twillingate & Beyond Tourism: Twillingate is known as the "Iceberg Capital of the World," and this tourism website provides information on tours, accommodations, and other activities in the area.
   https://www.visittwillingate.com/

3. Ocean Quest Adventures: This tour operator offers a variety of outdoor adventures in Newfoundland & Labrador, including iceberg and whale watching tours, scuba diving, and sea kayaking.
   https://oceanquestadventures.com/

4. Newfoundland & Labrador Tourism: The official tourism website for Newfoundland & Labrador provides information on all of the top activities and attractions in the province, including iceberg spotting.
https://www.newfoundlandlabrador.com/things-to-do/iceberg-viewing

Fishing and Hunting

Newfoundland & Labrador is known for its abundance of fishing and hunting opportunities, drawing anglers and hunters from around the world.

With over 29,000 kilometers of coastline and thousands of lakes and rivers, the province boasts an incredible variety of fish species, including Atlantic salmon, trout, cod, and more.

Hunting opportunities abound as well, with species such as moose, caribou, and black bear being popular targets.

Visitors can choose from a variety of fishing and hunting options, including guided tours and outfitters, as well as opportunities for independent fishing and hunting.

It's important to note that all non-residents of Canada are required to obtain a license before participating in any hunting or fishing activities. Links for fishing and hunting:

1. Fisheries and Oceans Canada - Recreational Fishing Regulations: https://www.dfo-mpo.gc.ca/fisheries-peches/recreational-recreative/index-eng.html
2. Government of Newfoundland & Labrador - Hunting and Trapping Guide: https://www.gov.nl.ca/hunting-trapping-guide/

Here are some tour guides for fishing and hunting in Newfoundland & Labrador:
1. Arluk Outfitters: https://www.arlukoutfitters.com/
2. Efford's Hunting Adventures: https://effordshunting.nf.ca/
3. Tuckamore Lodge: https://www.tuckamorelodge.com/
4. Indian Falls Chalets: https://www.indianfallschalets.com/

These tour guides offer a range of fishing and hunting experiences, from salmon fishing to big game hunting. Each has their own specialty and unique offerings, so it's worth checking out their websites to see which one would be the best fit for you.

Kayaking and Canoeing

Kayaking and canoeing are popular activities in Newfoundland and Labrador due to its many waterways and stunning coastline.

From serene lakes to rushing rivers and coastal inlets, the province offers many opportunities to explore by paddle. Kayakers and canoeists can spot wildlife, such as moose, caribou, and seabirds, and enjoy breathtaking scenery.

There are various guided kayaking and canoeing tours available throughout the province, from half-day trips to multi-day expeditions.

Some popular locations for kayaking and canoeing include Bonne Bay in Gros Morne National Park, the historic Exploits River, and the rugged coastlines of the East Coast Trail.

Here are some links to tour guides in Newfoundland & Labrador:

1. Gros Morne Adventures
   https://grosmorneadventures.com/

2. Explore Newfoundland
   https://www.explorenewfoundland.com/canoeing-and-kayaking/

3. The Outfitters Adventures
https://theoutfitters.nf.ca/

4. Wildland Tours
https://wildlands.com/home

5. Trinity Eco-Tours
https://trinityecotours.com/

These tour guides offer a range of kayaking and canoeing experiences, from short tours around the coast to multi-day trips through remote wilderness areas. They also provide all necessary gear and equipment, as well as experienced guides to ensure your safety and enjoyment on the water.

Snowmobiling and Skiing

Snowmobiling and skiing are popular winter activities in Newfoundland and Labrador. The province has many snowmobiling and skiing trails that offer a variety of terrains for different skill levels.

Snowmobiling is an exhilarating way to explore the snowy landscape, and many tours and rentals are available for visitors.

Skiing in Newfoundland and Labrador offers a unique experience as there are no ski resorts. Instead, visitors can ski on ungroomed backcountry trails or cross-country ski on groomed trails.

This provides a more authentic and rustic skiing experience for those who enjoy the outdoors.

There are also opportunities for heli-skiing in the province, which involves being flown to remote, untouched areas to ski down steep mountains.

Here are some links to snowmobiling and skiing information in Newfoundland and Labrador:
- Newfoundland and Labrador Snowmobile Association: https://nlsf.org/
- Cross Country Ski Newfoundland and Labrador: https://www.crosscountrynl.com/
- Marble Mountain Ski Resort: https://www.skimarble.com/
- Humber Valley Resort: https://www.humbervalley.com/

Here are some tour guide options for snowmobiling and skiing in Newfoundland and Labrador:

1. Marble Zip Tours (Snowmobiling): Offers snowmobiling tours through the backcountry of the Humber Valley, featuring stunning views and the chance to spot wildlife. https://www.marbleziptours.com/snowmobile-tours
2. Wild Gros Morne (Skiing): Offers guided backcountry skiing tours in Gros Morne National Park, with options for both beginner and experienced skiers. https://wildgrosmorne.com/

3. Backcountry Labrador (Snowmobiling): Offers multi-day snowmobile tours through the rugged wilderness of Labrador, featuring stunning scenery and the chance to see the northern lights.
4. Tuckamore Lodge (Skiing): Offers guided cross-country skiing tours through the beautiful forests and hills of the Northern Peninsula, with options for both classic and skate skiing.
5. Labrador Wildlands (Snowmobiling): Offers snowmobiling tours through the remote and untouched wilderness of Labrador, with options for both day trips and multi-day expeditions.
6. Canoe Hill Adventures (Skiing): Offers guided ski touring trips in the scenic Canoe Hill area, with options for both half-day and full-day tours.

Notes:

_____

_____

_____

Indigenous Groups Newfoundland and Labrador

Newfoundland and Labrador is home to several Indigenous groups, each with a rich cultural heritage and deep connections to the land. These groups have inhabited the region for thousands of years, leaving a lasting imprint on the history, traditions, and identity of the province. In this chapter, we will explore some of the Indigenous groups in Newfoundland and Labrador, their unique cultures, and their contributions to the region.

Innu Nation:

The Innu, also known as the Montagnais-Naskapi, are the Indigenous people of Labrador. They have a strong presence in the northern and central parts of Labrador and are known for their deep connection to the land and their traditional hunting and fishing practices. The Innu have a rich oral tradition, passing down stories and legends through generations. Today, the Innu Nation works to preserve their language, culture, and land rights, while also engaging in modern economic and social development.

Mi'kmaq:

The Mi'kmaq people have a long history in Newfoundland and Labrador, with roots dating back thousands of years. They are part of the larger Mi'kmaq Nation, which extends across the Atlantic provinces and Quebec. The Mi'kmaq have a strong connection to the land and sea, relying on hunting, fishing, and gathering for their sustenance. Their cultural practices include storytelling, drumming, and intricate beadwork. The Mi'kmaq continue to maintain their cultural traditions while also advocating for Indigenous rights and self-governance.

NunatuKavut Community Council:

The NunatuKavut Community Council represents the Inuit of southern Labrador, who are known as the Southern Inuit. They have a distinct cultural identity and have traditionally relied on hunting, fishing, and trapping for their livelihoods. The Southern Inuit have a close relationship with the natural environment and have a rich tradition of storytelling, throat singing, and drum dancing. The NunatuKavut Community Council works to promote Inuit culture, protect their land and resources, and address social and economic issues faced by their community.

Qalipu Mi'kmaq First Nation:

The Qalipu Mi'kmaq First Nation is a band located in western Newfoundland. It represents the Mi'kmaq people in this region, who have historical and ancestral ties to the area. The Qalipu Mi'kmaq First Nation is recognized as a status Indian band under the Indian Act and is actively engaged in preserving their cultural heritage, promoting Mi'kmaq language, and supporting community development initiatives.

These Indigenous groups have contributed significantly to the cultural fabric of Newfoundland and Labrador. They have preserved their unique traditions, languages, and customs, while also advocating for their rights, land claims, and self-determination. Visitors to the province can learn about their rich histories and cultures through various means, such as visiting Indigenous cultural centers, participating in cultural events, or engaging in Indigenous-led tourism experiences.

It is essential to acknowledge and respect the Indigenous peoples of Newfoundland and Labrador, honor their contributions, and support their ongoing efforts for cultural revitalization, self-governance, and community well-being. By fostering understanding and appreciation for Indigenous cultures, we can build stronger relationships and promote reconciliation within the province.

These links provide information on various Indigenous communities, organizations, and attractions related to Indigenous culture in Newfoundland and Labrador.

1. Qalipu First Nation - https://qalipu.ca/
2. Innu Nation - https://innu.ca/
3. NunatuKavut Community Council - https://www.nunatukavut.ca/
4. Nunatsiavut Government - https://www.nunatsiavut.com/
5. The Rooms - https://www.therooms.ca/
6. Red Ochre Gallery - https://www.redochregallery.ca/
7. Benoit First Nation - http://benoitfirstnation.ca/

The Vibrant Communities of Newfoundland & Labrador

Western Region & Northern Peninsula

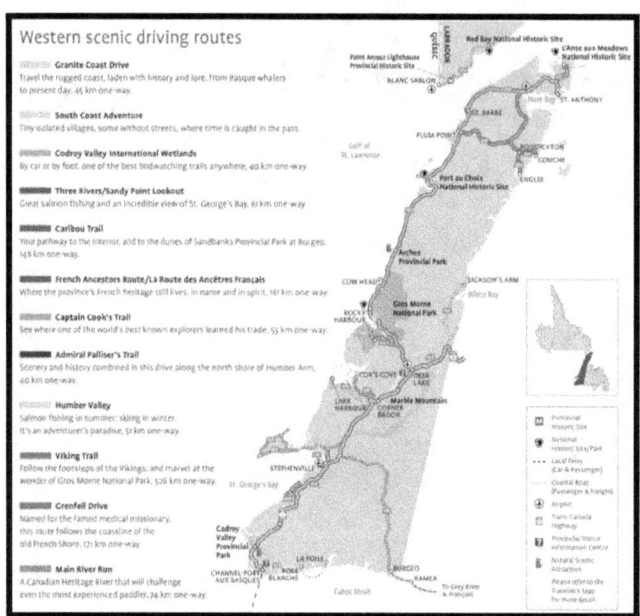

Port aux Basques

Port aux Basques is a picturesque coastal town located on the southwestern tip of Newfoundland's West Coast. Known as the gateway to the island, it serves as the primary ferry terminal connecting Newfoundland to mainland Canada. Here are some highlights of places to stay, eat, see, and outdoor activities in Port aux Basques:

Places to Stay:

Hotel Port aux Basques: This hotel offers comfortable rooms with modern amenities and is conveniently located near the ferry terminal.

St. Christopher's Hotel: A popular choice among visitors, St. Christopher's Hotel offers cozy accommodations, a restaurant, and friendly service. Local bed and breakfast establishments: Port aux Basques has several charming bed and breakfast options that provide a personalized experience and a chance to connect with the local community.

Places to Eat:

Harbour Restaurant & Lounge: Enjoy delicious seafood and traditional Newfoundland cuisine while overlooking the scenic harbor.

Seaview Restaurant: This family-friendly restaurant offers a diverse menu featuring fresh seafood, steaks, and hearty pub fare.

Port 7 Restaurant: Known for its warm hospitality, Port 7 serves up tasty comfort food with a focus on locally sourced ingredients.

Places to Visit:

Rose Blanche Lighthouse: A short drive from Port aux Basques, the Rose Blanche Lighthouse is a historic landmark perched atop rugged cliffs. Explore the museum and climb to the top for stunning views.

Channel Head Lighthouse: Located just outside of town, this iconic lighthouse stands as a symbol of the area's maritime heritage. Take a stroll along the coastline and enjoy the beautiful vistas.

Grand Bay West Beach: Relax on the sandy shores of this pristine beach, go for a swim, or take a leisurely walk along the shoreline.

Outdoor Activities:

Hiking: Lace up your hiking boots and explore scenic trails in the area, such as the Grand Bay West Trail, which offers panoramic views of the coastline and the Gulf of St. Lawrence.

Fishing: Join a local fishing charter and experience the thrill of reeling in cod, mackerel, or even a trophy-sized salmon.

Whale Watching: Embark on a boat tour from Port aux Basques to witness the majestic marine life, including humpback whales, dolphins, and seabirds.

Port aux Basques offers a warm welcome to travelers, with its stunning natural beauty, friendly locals, and a variety of accommodations, dining options, and outdoor activities to enhance your visit.

Corner Brook

Nestled among the scenic hills and rivers of western Newfoundland, Corner Brook is a vibrant city known for its stunning natural beauty and outdoor recreational opportunities. Here are some highlights of places to stay, eat, see, and outdoor activities in Corner Brook:

Places to Stay:

Glynmill Inn: This historic Tudor-style inn offers comfortable rooms with a touch of old-world charm. It's conveniently located near downtown Corner Brook and features a renowned restaurant and lounge.

Greenwood Inn & Suites: A modern hotel with spacious rooms, amenities like a fitness center and indoor pool, and a popular on-site restaurant. Vacation rentals: Corner Brook offers a range of vacation rental options, including cabins and cottages, providing a cozy and private retreat for visitors.

Places to Eat:

Newfound Sushi: Indulge in delicious sushi rolls, fresh sashimi, and other Japanese-inspired dishes at this popular restaurant.

Saltbox Kitchen: Located in a charming saltbox house, this eatery offers a unique dining experience with a focus on locally sourced ingredients and creative menus.

Brewed Awakening: A cozy café known for its artisanal coffee, baked goods, and light fare, perfect for a quick bite or a relaxing afternoon.

Places to Visit:

Marble Mountain: Just outside of Corner Brook, Marble Mountain is a renowned ski resort offering exhilarating winter sports and breathtaking views. In the summer, enjoy scenic chairlift rides, hiking, and mountain biking trails.

Captain James Cook Historic Site: Visit the monument and interpretive center dedicated to the famous British explorer Captain James Cook, who surveyed the region in the 18th century.

Corner Brook Museum and Archives: Explore the rich history and cultural heritage of Corner Brook through exhibits and artifacts showcasing the area's past.

Outdoor Activities:

Humber Valley: Discover the natural beauty of the Humber Valley through hiking and walking trails that wind through lush forests, along rushing rivers, and past stunning waterfalls.

Gros Morne National Park: While technically located outside of Corner Brook, Gros Morne is a must-visit destination nearby. Explore its fjords, hike the iconic Gros Morne Mountain, and experience the park's diverse ecosystems and geological wonders.

Kayaking and Canoeing: Take to the waters of Corner Brook's nearby lakes and rivers for a peaceful paddle surrounded by picturesque landscapes.

Corner Brook offers a blend of urban amenities and access to pristine natural wonders, making it an ideal destination for outdoor enthusiasts and those seeking cultural experiences. With its cozy accommodations, diverse dining options, and exciting outdoor activities, Corner Brook provides a memorable Newfoundland and Labrador experience.

Rocky Harbour (Gros Morne)

Rocky Harbour is a charming coastal town situated within the breathtaking Gros Morne National Park on Newfoundland's West Coast. Surrounded by stunning landscapes, this community offers a perfect base for exploring the park's natural wonders. Here are some highlights of places to stay, eat, see, and outdoor activities in Rocky Harbour:

Places to Stay:

Ocean View Hotel: Located near the waterfront, this hotel provides comfortable rooms with picturesque views of Bonne Bay. It also features a restaurant and lounge offering local cuisine.

Fisherman's Landing Inn: A cozy inn with comfortable accommodations and a warm, welcoming atmosphere. It offers a convenient location within walking distance of local amenities.

Vacation rentals: There are various vacation rentals available in Rocky Harbour, including cottages and cabins, providing visitors with a home-away-from-home experience.

Places to Eat:

The Black Spruce Restaurant: Enjoy delicious seafood, traditional Newfoundland dishes, and other regional specialties at this popular restaurant. The cozy atmosphere and friendly service make it a favorite among locals and visitors alike.

The Old Loft Restaurant: Set in a restored heritage building, this restaurant offers a unique dining experience with a menu that highlights fresh, local ingredients and creative culinary techniques.

Java Jack's: A cozy coffee shop and café where you can savor a variety of freshly brewed coffees, baked goods, light meals, and sandwiches.

Places to Visit:

Gros Morne National Park Visitor Centre: Learn about the park's natural and cultural heritage at the visitor center, which offers exhibits, interactive displays, and information on hiking trails and guided tours.

Western Brook Pond: Take a boat tour of this stunning fjord, surrounded by towering cliffs and cascading waterfalls. The boat tour provides a unique perspective of the park's beauty.

Lobster Cove Head Lighthouse: Visit this picturesque lighthouse, perched on rugged cliffs overlooking the Atlantic Ocean. Explore the interpretive center and enjoy panoramic views of the coastline.

Outdoor Activities:

Hiking: Gros Morne National Park offers an extensive network of hiking trails, catering to various skill levels. The Tablelands, Gros Morne Mountain, and Green Gardens are popular hiking destinations within the park.

Kayaking: Experience the tranquility of Bonne Bay or explore the coastal waters surrounding Rocky Harbour on a guided kayaking excursion.

Wildlife Viewing: Keep an eye out for wildlife such as moose, caribou, foxes, and a variety of bird species as you explore the park's trails and scenic viewpoints.

Rocky Harbour serves as an ideal gateway to the wonders of Gros Morne National Park. With its comfortable accommodations, diverse dining options, and numerous outdoor activities, this town offers an unforgettable experience for nature lovers and adventurers.

Norris Point (Gros Morne)

Nestled within the spectacular Gros Morne National Park on Newfoundland's West Coast, Norris Point is a picturesque village known for its stunning natural beauty and outdoor adventures.

Surrounded by breathtaking landscapes, this community offers a tranquil escape for nature enthusiasts. Here are some highlights of places to stay, eat, see, and outdoor activities in Norris Point:

Places to Stay:

Bonne Bay Inn: A charming waterfront inn offering comfortable rooms with scenic views of Bonne Bay. The inn features a restaurant, lounge, and cozy common areas.

Sugar Hill Inn: This cozy bed and breakfast provides comfortable accommodations and warm hospitality. Enjoy a hearty breakfast and relax in the peaceful surroundings.

Vacation Rentals: Norris Point offers a range of vacation rentals, including cabins and cottages, providing visitors with a private and serene retreat amidst nature.

Places to Eat:

The Cat Stop Pub & Grub: A popular local pub serving up delicious pub fare, including burgers, fish and chips, and other tasty dishes. Enjoy a cold drink and live music in a friendly atmosphere.

Java Jack's: Located at the BonTours Boat Tour Office, Java Jack's is a great spot for a coffee break or a light meal. Try their freshly brewed coffee, sandwiches, and baked goods.

The Old Store Cafe: This cozy cafe offers a delightful menu featuring homemade soups, sandwiches, and baked goods. Sit back, relax, and savor the flavors while enjoying views of the surrounding nature.

Places to Visit:

BonTours Boat Tours: Embark on a scenic boat tour of Bonne Bay, where you can marvel at the towering cliffs, waterfalls, and abundant wildlife. Keep an eye out for whales, seabirds, and even bald eagles.

Tablelands: Take a guided hike or explore on your own in the Tablelands, a unique geological formation with exposed mantle rock. The rust-colored terrain offers a stark contrast to the lush greenery of the park.

Jenniex House: Visit this charming historic house, which has been transformed into a small museum that showcases the area's cultural heritage and the traditional way of life.

Outdoor Activities:

Hiking: Explore the numerous hiking trails in Gros Morne National Park, including the scenic Green Gardens Trail, the Lookout Trail with panoramic views, or the challenging Gros Morne Mountain Trail.

Kayaking and Paddleboarding: Rent a kayak or paddleboard and explore the calm waters of Bonne Bay, immersing yourself in the tranquility of the surroundings.

Birdwatching: Gros Morne National Park is a haven for birdwatchers. Keep an eye out for a variety of bird species, including eagles, puffins, and ospreys.

Norris Point offers a serene and idyllic setting for nature lovers and adventure seekers. With its cozy accommodations, local eateries, breathtaking sights, and outdoor activities, it provides an unforgettable experience in the heart of Gros Morne National Park.

Woody Point (Gros Morne)

Woody Point is a charming community located in Gros Morne National Park on Newfoundland's West Coast.

Known for its scenic beauty, rich history, and cultural attractions, Woody Point offers visitors a unique and immersive experience.

Here are some highlights of places to stay, eat, see, and outdoor activities in Woody Point:

Places to Stay:

The Old Saltbox Co.: Experience the charm of a traditional Newfoundland saltbox house by staying in one of The Old Saltbox Co.'s beautifully restored vacation homes. These cozy and fully equipped accommodations provide a glimpse into local heritage while offering modern comforts.

Gros Morne Cabins: Nestled amidst the pristine wilderness of Gros Morne National Park, Gros Morne Cabins offers rustic yet comfortable cabins with stunning views of the surrounding landscape. Unplug from the world and enjoy the tranquility of nature.

Gros Morne Suites: Located in the heart of Woody Point, Gros Morne Suites offers spacious and well-appointed suites with modern amenities. Enjoy the convenience of being close to local attractions and services.

Places to Eat:

The Loft Restaurant: Situated in a historic building, The Loft Restaurant serves up delicious meals made with locally sourced ingredients. Enjoy traditional Newfoundland dishes, seafood specialties, and stunning views of Bonne Bay.

The Black Spruce: This cozy café offers a warm and inviting atmosphere along with a menu that features homemade soups, sandwiches, and baked goods. Indulge in a cup of coffee or tea while savoring the local flavors.

The Merchant Warehouse: Housed in a restored heritage building, The Merchant Warehouse is a popular spot for dining and drinks. Enjoy a diverse menu that includes pub fare, seafood, and vegetarian options, accompanied by a selection of local craft beers.

Places to Visit:

Bonne Bay Marine Station: Visit the Bonne Bay Marine Station, a research and education facility that showcases the diverse marine life of the area. Explore the touch tanks, exhibits, and interpretive displays to learn about the fascinating ecosystems of Newfoundland's waters.

Woody Point Heritage Theatre: Experience live entertainment, music, and theater performances at the Woody Point Heritage Theatre. This restored community theater is a cultural hub and hosts a variety of events throughout the year.

Woody Point Walking Trail: Take a leisurely stroll along the Woody Point Walking Trail, which offers beautiful views of the town, Bonne Bay, and the surrounding mountains. Enjoy the fresh air and immerse yourself in the natural beauty of the area.

Outdoor Activities:

Hiking: Explore the scenic hiking trails in Gros Morne National Park, such as the Green Gardens Trail or the Gros Morne Mountain Trail. Marvel at the rugged landscapes, panoramic views, and unique geological formations.

Kayaking: Rent a kayak and paddle along the calm waters of Bonne Bay, enjoying the serenity of the surroundings and the possibility of wildlife sightings. Boat Tours: Embark on a boat tour to explore the stunning fjords, waterfalls, and coastal scenery of Bonne Bay. Learn about the geological and cultural history of the area while enjoying the breathtaking views.

Woody Point offers a blend of natural beauty, cultural experiences, and outdoor adventures in the heart of Gros Morne National Park. With its range of accommodations, dining options, and opportunities for exploration, Woody Point provides a memorable and immersive experience for visitors seeking to connect with nature and local heritage.

Bonne Bay (Gros Morne)

Bonne Bay is a scenic area located within Gros Morne National Park on Newfoundland's West Coast. Known for its stunning fjords, rugged landscapes, and diverse wildlife, Bonne Bay offers a range of experiences for nature lovers and outdoor enthusiasts.

Here are some highlights of places to stay, eat, see, and outdoor activities in Bonne Bay:

Places to Stay:

Neddies Harbour Inn: Situated on the shores of Bonne Bay, Neddies Harbour Inn offers luxurious accommodations with breathtaking views. Experience warm hospitality, elegant rooms, and a gourmet dining experience at their on-site restaurant.

Sugar Hill Inn: Nestled on a hill overlooking Bonne Bay, Sugar Hill Inn provides cozy rooms with rustic charm. Enjoy the tranquil setting, homemade breakfast, and personalized service.

Campgrounds: For those seeking a more immersive outdoor experience, there are several campgrounds within Gros Morne National Park, including Lomond, Berry Hill, and Shallow Bay campgrounds. These offer opportunities to camp amidst nature's beauty.

Places to Eat:

The Old Loft Restaurant: Located in Rocky Harbour, near Bonne Bay, The Old Loft Restaurant features a menu that highlights local seafood, game, and traditional Newfoundland dishes. Enjoy a fine dining experience with stunning views of the bay.

Java Jack's Restaurant & Gallery: Situated in Norris Point, Java Jack's is a cozy café known for its delicious coffee, homemade baked goods, and light meals. Take a break and savor their treats while enjoying the scenic surroundings.

Bonne Bay Inn & Seaside Suites: This waterfront inn and restaurant offer a unique dining experience, featuring fresh seafood, locally sourced ingredients, and a warm, inviting atmosphere.

Places to Visit:

Western Brook Pond: Take a boat tour or hike to the stunning Western Brook Pond, a glacier-carved fjord surrounded by towering cliffs and waterfalls. Explore this natural wonder and be captivated by its awe-inspiring beauty.

The Tablelands: Witness the unique geological landscape of The Tablelands, a mountainous region with exposed Earth's mantle. Take a hike and learn about the rare plant species that thrive in this unusual environment.

Bonne Bay Marine Station: Visit the Bonne Bay Marine Station, a research and education facility that offers interactive exhibits and displays about the marine life and ecosystems found in Bonne Bay.

Outdoor Activities:

Hiking: Explore the numerous hiking trails in and around Bonne Bay, such as the Lookout Trail, Berry Hill Pond Trail, or the Green Gardens Trail. Each trail offers unique vistas, wildlife sightings, and opportunities to connect with nature.

Kayaking and Canoeing: Rent a kayak or canoe and paddle through the calm waters of Bonne Bay, exploring its hidden coves, secluded beaches, and observing marine life up close.

Wildlife Watching: Keep an eye out for wildlife such as moose, caribou, foxes, and various bird species that inhabit the area. Wildlife viewing opportunities are plentiful within Gros Morne National Park.

Bonne Bay offers a blend of natural wonders, outdoor adventures, and opportunities to immerse yourself in the beauty of Gros Morne National Park. Whether you choose to stay in a cozy inn, indulge in local cuisine, explore scenic attractions, or partake in outdoor activities, Bonne Bay provides a memorable experience for visitors seeking to connect with nature's splendor.

Cow Head (Gros Morne)

Cow Head is a charming community located within Gros Morne National Park on Newfoundland's West Coast. Known for its stunning coastal beauty, rich cultural heritage, and proximity to remarkable natural attractions, Cow Head offers visitors a delightful combination of relaxation and outdoor adventure. Here are some highlights of places to stay, eat, see, and outdoor activities in Cow Head:

Places to Stay:

Shallow Bay Motel & Cabins: Situated near the shores of Shallow Bay, this accommodation offers comfortable motel rooms and cozy cabins with picturesque views. Enjoy the proximity to the beach and easy access to hiking trails.

Gros Morne RV Campground: If you prefer camping or traveling with an RV, the Gros Morne RV Campground in Cow Head provides spacious sites and basic amenities in a beautiful natural setting.

Seaside Suites: Experience tranquility by staying in one of the seaside suites available in Cow Head. These self-contained units offer stunning views of the ocean and convenient access to nearby attractions.

Places to Eat:

The Old Store Café: Located in a historic building, The Old Store Café offers a cozy atmosphere and a menu featuring homemade soups, sandwiches, and baked goods. It's an excellent spot to relax and enjoy a meal or a cup of coffee.

Ocean View Restaurant: Situated within Shallow Bay Motel, the Ocean View Restaurant serves up delicious seafood dishes and other local specialties. Enjoy your meal while taking in the panoramic views of the bay.

Woody Point Bakery & Café: Although not in Cow Head itself, the Woody Point Bakery & Café, located nearby, is worth a visit. Sample their freshly baked goods, sandwiches, and coffee in a quaint and inviting setting.

Places to Visit:

Cow Head Lighthouse: Visit the picturesque Cow Head Lighthouse, perched on a rocky outcrop overlooking the Gulf of St. Lawrence. Take in the breathtaking views and learn about the importance of lighthouses in the region's maritime history.

Gros Morne Theatre Festival: Enjoy live theater performances at the Gros Morne Theatre Festival, located in Cow Head. Experience the rich cultural heritage of the area through entertaining plays, music, and storytelling.

Arches Provincial Park: Just a short drive from Cow Head, Arches Provincial Park showcases magnificent natural rock arches formed by coastal erosion. Take a leisurely walk along the trails and marvel at the impressive geological formations.

Outdoor Activities:

Hiking: Explore the numerous hiking trails in the vicinity, such as the Cow Head Walking Trail or the nearby Green Point Geological Site. Immerse yourself in the stunning coastal landscapes, unique rock formations, and lush forests.

Beachcombing: Take a leisurely stroll along Shallow Bay Beach, known for its sandy shores and scenic beauty. Enjoy beachcombing for seashells and other treasures, or simply relax and soak up the peaceful atmosphere.

Whale Watching: Embark on a whale watching tour from nearby communities, such as Rocky Harbour or Norris Point, and witness the majestic humpback whales that frequent the waters of the Gulf of St. Lawrence.

Cow Head provides a serene and picturesque setting for visitors to Gros Morne National Park. Whether you choose to stay in a cozy cabin, indulge in local cuisine, explore scenic attractions, or engage in outdoor activities, Cow Head offers a memorable experience for those seeking a blend of natural beauty and cultural immersion.

Woody Point (Gros Morne)

Woody Point is a picturesque community located in Gros Morne National Park on the West Coast of Newfoundland and Labrador. Known for its stunning natural beauty, rich cultural heritage, and charming atmosphere, Woody Point offers a range of experiences for visitors.

Here are some highlights of places to stay, eat, see, and outdoor activities in Woody Point:

Places to Stay:

The Old Salt Box Co.: Experience the charm of a traditional saltbox house by staying at The Old Salt Box Co. They offer cozy vacation rentals with rustic decor and modern amenities, providing a comfortable and authentic Newfoundland experience.

Woody Point Heritage Theatre: Stay in one of the suites located within the Woody Point Heritage Theatre. These accommodations offer a unique blend of comfort and historic charm, with convenient access to live performances and events.

Places to Eat:

The Loft Restaurant: Located within the Woody Point Heritage Theatre, The Loft Restaurant serves delicious seafood dishes, hearty pub-style meals, and offers a selection of craft beers and spirits.

Enjoy your meal while taking in the stunning views of Bonne Bay.

The Black Spruce Restaurant & Bar: Situated in the heart of Woody Point, The Black Spruce Restaurant & Bar features a diverse menu of local and international cuisine. Enjoy their signature dishes, such as fresh seafood, steaks, and vegetarian options, in a warm and inviting atmosphere.

Places to Visit:

Bonne Bay: Take a leisurely stroll along the waterfront of Bonne Bay and soak in the breathtaking views of the bay, the surrounding hills, and the iconic Tablelands. Enjoy the tranquility of the area and watch for wildlife, including seabirds and whales.

The Heritage Theatre: Visit the Woody Point Heritage Theatre, a beautifully restored 1915 vaudeville hall that now hosts a variety of live performances, concerts, and cultural events. Immerse yourself in the rich artistic and cultural heritage of the region.

Writers at Woody Point: If you visit during the Writers at Woody Point literary festival, you can attend author readings, panel discussions, and musical performances featuring renowned Canadian and international artists.

Outdoor Activities:

Hiking: Explore the scenic hiking trails in Gros Morne National Park, including the nearby Discovery Centre Trail, Burnt Hill Trail, or the Lookout Trail. Enjoy panoramic views of the surrounding landscapes, forests, and coastline.

Kayaking and Canoeing: Rent a kayak or canoe and paddle along the tranquil waters of Bonne Bay, exploring the hidden coves, inlets, and wildlife-rich areas. Experience the serenity of the bay and marvel at the beauty of the surrounding cliffs.

Boat Tours: Embark on a boat tour from Woody Point and venture into the waters of Bonne Bay. Enjoy guided tours that highlight the natural wonders of the area, including the chance to see marine wildlife, waterfalls, and stunning geological formations.

Woody Point offers a unique blend of natural beauty, cultural experiences, and outdoor adventures within the breathtaking setting of Gros Morne National Park.

Whether you choose to stay in a cozy vacation rental, savor local cuisine, explore scenic attractions, or engage in outdoor activities, Woody Point provides a memorable and enchanting experience for visitors seeking to immerse themselves in the wonders of Newfoundland and Labrador.

St. Anthony (Northern Peninsula)

St. Anthony is a vibrant town located on the Northern Peninsula of Newfoundland and Labrador. It is known for its breathtaking landscapes, rich history, and proximity to stunning natural wonders.

Here are some highlights of places to stay, eat, see, and outdoor activities in St. Anthony:

Places to Stay:

Grenfell Heritage Hotel & Suites: This historic hotel offers comfortable accommodations with a touch of heritage charm. Enjoy modern amenities, friendly service, and convenient access to local attractions.

Haven Inn: Located near the waterfront, Haven Inn provides comfortable rooms and suites with beautiful views of the surrounding area. It offers a restaurant and lounge where you can unwind and enjoy a meal or drink.

Viking RV Park & Campground: For those who prefer camping or traveling with an RV, Viking RV Park & Campground offers spacious sites, amenities, and a peaceful natural setting.

Places to Eat:

The Norseman Restaurant & Gaia Art Gallery: Indulge in a delightful dining experience at The

Norseman Restaurant, known for its delicious seafood, steaks, and homemade desserts. The adjacent Gaia Art Gallery showcases local artwork and crafts.

Northern Delight Restaurant: This family-owned restaurant offers a warm and welcoming atmosphere and serves up a variety of dishes, including seafood, burgers, and vegetarian options.

Dockside Restaurant: Located near the waterfront, Dockside Restaurant offers panoramic views of St. Anthony Harbour and serves fresh seafood dishes, homemade soups, and other local specialties.

Places to Visit:

L'Anse aux Meadows National Historic Site: Explore the only authenticated Norse settlement in North America, a UNESCO World Heritage Site. Walk through reconstructed Viking buildings and learn about the Norse exploration and settlement in the area.

Grenfell Historic Properties: Visit the Grenfell Historic Properties, which includes the Grenfell House Museum and the Grenfell Interpretation Centre. Discover the fascinating legacy of Sir Wilfred Grenfell, a medical missionary who made significant contributions to the region.

Iceberg Viewing: During the iceberg season (typically from May to July), take a boat tour or hike along the coast to witness the awe-inspiring beauty of icebergs as they float by. Marvel at their majestic presence and vibrant colors.

Outdoor Activities:

Whale Watching: Embark on a whale watching tour and witness the magnificent humpback whales and other marine wildlife that frequent the waters of the Northern Peninsula. Experience the thrill of seeing these gentle giants up close.

Hiking: Explore the scenic hiking trails in the area, such as the Fishing Point Park Trail and the Tea House Hill Trail. Enjoy stunning views of the coastline, rugged cliffs, and the surrounding wilderness.

Fishing: St. Anthony is a popular destination for fishing enthusiasts. Join a guided fishing excursion and try your hand at catching Atlantic salmon, trout, or Arctic char in the pristine rivers and lakes of the region.

St. Anthony offers a blend of history, natural beauty, and outdoor adventures on the Northern Peninsula.

Whether you choose to stay in a heritage hotel, savor local cuisine, explore historic sites, or engage in outdoor activities, St. Anthony provides a memorable experience for visitors seeking to immerse themselves in the wonders of Newfoundland and Labrador.

L'Anse aux Meadows (Viking Settlement, Northern Peninsula)

L'Anse aux Meadows is an extraordinary archaeological site located on the Northern Peninsula of Newfoundland and Labrador. It is renowned for being the only authenticated Viking settlement in North America, dating back over a thousand years.

Here are some highlights of places to stay, eat, see, and outdoor activities in L'Anse aux Meadows:

Places to Stay:

Viking Village B&B: Experience Viking-themed accommodations at the Viking Village B&B, located near the historic site. Stay in cozy rooms inspired by Norse culture and enjoy warm hospitality and a delicious breakfast.

Burnt Cape Cabins: Located in nearby Raleigh, Burnt Cape Cabins offer charming cabins with modern amenities, nestled amidst the scenic beauty of the region. Immerse yourself in nature and enjoy the tranquility of the surroundings.

Tuckamore Lodge: If you're looking for a luxurious wilderness retreat, Tuckamore Lodge is an excellent choice. Situated in Main Brook, it offers upscale accommodations, gourmet meals, and guided outdoor activities.

Places to Eat:

Norseman Restaurant: Located at the Viking Village B&B, the Norseman Restaurant provides a unique dining experience inspired by Viking cuisine. Enjoy dishes that incorporate local ingredients and traditional flavors.

The Daily Catch: This cozy seafood restaurant in Raleigh serves up fresh and delicious fish and chips, lobster, and other local specialties. Enjoy a casual dining experience with a focus on seafood delights.

Snow's Takeout: If you're looking for a quick and tasty meal, Snow's Takeout in nearby Straitsview is a popular spot. They offer a variety of comfort foods, including burgers, poutine, and fried chicken.

Places to Visit:

L'Anse aux Meadows National Historic Site: Explore the UNESCO World Heritage Site of L'Anse aux Meadows, where the remains of the Viking settlement were discovered.

Visit reconstructed Norse buildings, see artifacts, and learn about the fascinating history of the Vikings in North America.

Norstead Viking Village: Adjacent to the historic site, Norstead Viking Village is a living history attraction that provides an immersive Viking experience. Engage in interactive demonstrations, watch reenactments, and learn about Viking culture and craftsmanship.

Burnt Cape Ecological Reserve: Take a short drive to the nearby Burnt Cape Ecological Reserve, known for its unique and rare plant species. Explore the boardwalks and trails that wind through this beautiful coastal landscape.

Outdoor Activities:

Hiking: Discover the natural beauty of the area by hiking along the rugged coastal trails. Enjoy scenic vistas, rocky shorelines, and the fresh coastal air. The Iceberg Trail and the T'Railway Provincial Park are popular options.

Whale Watching: Join a boat tour or keep an eye out from the shore for the chance to witness majestic whales, such as humpbacks or minke whales, as they migrate through the waters near L'Anse aux Meadows.

Birdwatching: The Northern Peninsula is a haven for birdwatchers. Look out for seabirds, shorebirds, and various species of songbirds that inhabit the region. The Long Point Lighthouse is a prime birdwatching spot.

L'Anse aux Meadows offers a remarkable journey into the Viking history of North America. Whether you choose to stay in Viking-themed accommodations, indulge in local cuisine, explore historic sites, or engage in outdoor activities, L'Anse aux Meadows provides a truly immersive and unforgettable experience.

Deer Lake

Deer Lake is a vibrant town located on Newfoundland's West Coast, known for its scenic beauty, friendly atmosphere, and proximity to outdoor adventures. Surrounded by stunning wilderness and situated near Gros Morne National Park, Deer Lake offers a range of options for places to stay, eat, see, and engage in outdoor activities.

Places to Stay:

Holiday Inn Express Deer Lake: This modern hotel offers comfortable rooms, complimentary breakfast, and amenities like a fitness center and indoor pool. It's conveniently located near the airport and offers easy access to the town's attractions.

Humber Valley Resort: For a luxurious stay, consider the Humber Valley Resort, which features beautiful chalets and villas nestled in the picturesque Humber Valley. Enjoy golfing, spa services, and stunning views of the surrounding landscape.

Bed and Breakfast establishments: Deer Lake has several cozy bed and breakfast accommodations that provide a personalized touch and a chance to connect with the local community.

Places to Eat:

Newfound Sushi: Indulge in a variety of sushi rolls, sashimi, and other Japanese dishes at this popular restaurant, which offers fresh and flavorful options for seafood lovers.

Wings Tap & Grill: Known for its wings and pub-style fare, this casual restaurant is a favorite spot for locals and visitors alike. Enjoy a wide selection of wing flavors and other tasty dishes.

The Driftwood Restaurant: This family-friendly restaurant offers a diverse menu featuring seafood, steaks, burgers, and comfort food classics. Don't miss out on their delicious homemade desserts.

Places to Visit:

Newfoundland Insectarium & Butterfly Pavilion: Explore the fascinating world of insects and butterflies at this unique attraction. Discover a variety of species, learn about their habitats, and even interact with live butterflies.

Roy Whelan Heritage Museum & Valley Crafts: Immerse yourself in the rich history and culture of the region at this museum. View exhibits on local heritage, crafts, and traditional artifacts.

Deer Lake Beach: Spend a relaxing day at Deer Lake Beach, where you can swim, sunbathe, and enjoy picnics by the water. The beach offers beautiful views of the surrounding mountains.

Outdoor Activities:

Hiking and Nature Trails: Deer Lake is a gateway to numerous hiking and nature trails, offering scenic vistas, wildlife viewing opportunities, and a chance to immerse yourself in the natural beauty of the area. Explore trails like the Humber River Nature Trail or nearby trails in Gros Morne National Park.

Canoeing and Kayaking: Rent a canoe or kayak and paddle along the serene waters of Deer Lake or nearby rivers, enjoying the tranquility and beautiful surroundings.

Fishing: Cast your line and try your luck at catching trout or salmon in the abundant rivers and lakes in the region. Fishing enthusiasts will find plenty of opportunities for a rewarding angling experience.

Deer Lake combines natural beauty with modern amenities, making it an excellent base for exploring the surrounding wilderness and enjoying outdoor activities. With its range of accommodations, dining options, and recreational opportunities, Deer Lake offers a memorable experience for travelers seeking adventure and relaxation.

Central Region

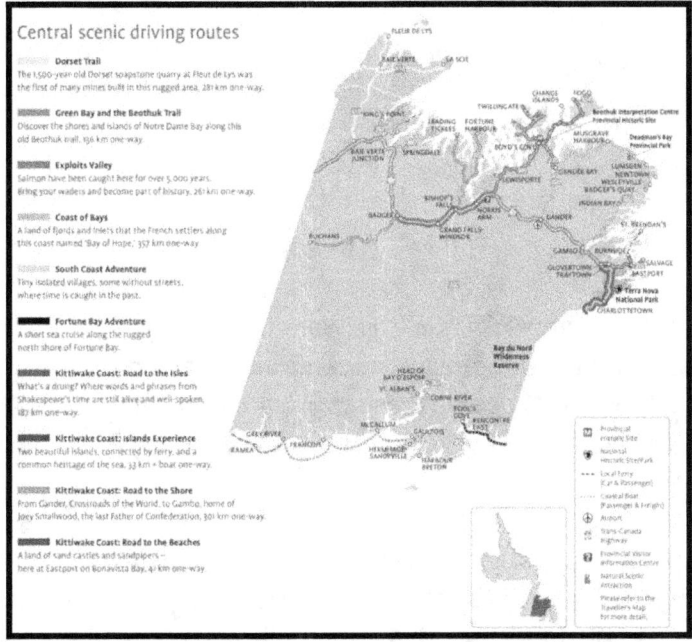

Central scenic driving routes

Dorset Trail
The 1,500-year-old Dorset soapstone quarry at Fleur de Lys was the first of many mines built in this rugged area. 281 km one-way.

Green Bay and the Beothuk Trail
Discover the shores and islands of Notre Dame Bay along this old Beothuk trail. 156 km one-way.

Exploits Valley
Salmon have been caught here for over 5,000 years. Bring your waders and become part of history. 261 km one-way.

Coast of Bays
A land of fjords and inlets that the French settlers along this coast named 'Bay of Hope.' 357 km one-way.

South Coast Adventure
Tiny isolated villages, some without streets, where time is caught in the past.

Fortune Bay Adventure
A short sea cruise along the rugged north shore of Fortune Bay.

Kittiwake Coast: Road to the Isles
What's a drung? Where words and phrases from Shakespeare's time are still alive and well-spoken. 182 km one-way.

Kittiwake Coast: Islands Experience
Two beautiful islands, connected by ferry, and a common heritage of the sea. 53 km + boat one-way.

Kittiwake Coast: Road to the Shore
From Gander, Crossroads of the World, to Gambo, home of Joey Smallwood, the last Father of Confederation. 301 km one-way.

Kittiwake Coast: Road to the Beaches
A land of sand castles and sandpipers – here at Eastport on Bonavista Bay. 41 km one-way.

Twillingate

Twillingate is a charming town located in the Central region of Newfoundland and Labrador. Known as the "Iceberg Capital of the World," it offers breathtaking coastal scenery, vibrant culture, and a range of outdoor activities.

Here are some highlights of places to stay, eat, see, and outdoor activities in Twillingate:

Places to Stay:

Anchor Inn Hotel & Suites: This waterfront hotel offers comfortable rooms with scenic views of the ocean. It provides easy access to local attractions and features an on-site restaurant, lounge, and gift shop.

The Wilds at Salmonier River: Located just outside Twillingate, The Wilds at Salmonier River offers luxurious cottages nestled in a tranquil wilderness setting. Enjoy spacious accommodations, modern amenities, and access to outdoor activities.

Places to Eat:

Auk Island Winery: Sample locally made wines and indulge in delicious meals at Auk Island Winery's on-site restaurant. Enjoy fresh seafood, local specialties, and stunning views of the coastline.
Twillingate Fish Market: Savor fresh seafood at the Twillingate Fish Market, where you can enjoy fish

and chips, lobster, crab, and other delectable seafood dishes.

The Crow's Nest Café & Suites: This café offers a cozy atmosphere and serves homemade meals, including sandwiches, soups, and desserts. They also offer comfortable suites for overnight stays.

Places to Visit:

Long Point Lighthouse: Visit the iconic Long Point Lighthouse, which overlooks Twillingate Harbour. Enjoy panoramic views of the coastline, surrounding islands, and the chance to spot icebergs and whales.

Prime Berth Fishing Museum: Explore the Prime Berth Fishing Museum, which showcases the area's rich fishing heritage. Learn about traditional fishing methods, view historic artifacts, and interact with knowledgeable guides.

Twillingate Museum & Crafts: Discover the history and culture of Twillingate at the Twillingate Museum. Explore exhibits that highlight the town's past, including its fishing industry, iceberg sightings, and famous residents.

Outdoor Activities:

Iceberg and Whale Watching: Take a boat tour and witness the awe-inspiring sight of icebergs floating along Twillingate's coast. Depending on the season, you may also have the opportunity to spot majestic whales, such as humpbacks or minke whales.

Hiking: Explore the scenic hiking trails in the area, such as the French Beach Trail or the Spiller's Cove Trail. Enjoy breathtaking coastal views, rugged cliffs, and the chance to spot wildlife along the way.

Sea Kayaking: Rent a kayak or join a guided sea kayaking tour to explore Twillingate's coastline up close. Paddle through pristine waters, discover hidden coves, and admire the natural beauty of the area.

Twillingate offers a captivating blend of natural wonders, cultural experiences, and outdoor adventures in the heart of Newfoundland and Labrador's Central region.

Whether you choose to stay in a waterfront hotel, indulge in local cuisine, explore historic sites, or engage in outdoor activities, Twillingate provides a memorable and enchanting experience for visitors seeking to immerse themselves in the beauty of this coastal gem.

Fogo Island

Fogo Island is a captivating island located in the Central region of Newfoundland and Labrador. Renowned for its rugged landscapes, vibrant culture, and unique architecture, Fogo Island offers a one-of-a-kind experience for visitors.

Here are some highlights of places to stay, eat, see, and outdoor activities in Fogo Island:

Places to Stay:

Fogo Island Inn: This award-winning, contemporary inn is a masterpiece of architecture and design. It offers luxurious accommodations with stunning views of the North Atlantic Ocean. Enjoy world-class amenities, locally sourced cuisine, and access to cultural experiences.

Quirpon Lighthouse Inn: Located on a remote island off the northern tip of Fogo Island, Quirpon Lighthouse Inn offers a truly unique experience. Stay in cozy accommodations within a restored lighthouse and immerse yourself in the tranquil beauty of the surroundings.

Places to Eat:

Nicole's Café: Indulge in delicious meals at Nicole's Café, which focuses on using fresh, local ingredients. Savor dishes inspired by Newfoundland and Labrador's culinary traditions, including seafood specialties and homemade desserts.

The Inn Kitchen at Fogo Island Inn: Experience fine dining at The Inn Kitchen, the renowned restaurant within Fogo Island Inn. Enjoy a seasonal menu featuring local and foraged ingredients, prepared by talented chefs.

Places to Visit:

Fogo Island Arts: Visit the Fogo Island Arts gallery, which showcases contemporary art from local and international artists. Explore exhibitions that highlight the island's cultural heritage and artistic creativity.

Fogo Island Marine Interpretation Centre: Learn about the marine ecosystems and cultural history of Fogo Island at the Marine Interpretation Centre. Discover exhibits, interactive displays, and educational programs that showcase the island's maritime heritage.

Joe Batt's Arm: Explore the picturesque fishing village of Joe Batt's Arm, known for its colorful houses and scenic beauty. Take a leisurely stroll along the harbor, interact with locals, and immerse yourself in the community's rich culture.

Outdoor Activities:

Hiking and Nature Walks: Explore the island's natural beauty by hiking along the many trails available, such as the Brimstone Head Trail or the Lion's Den Trail. Enjoy panoramic views, encounter wildlife, and immerse yourself in the serene surroundings.

Kayaking and Boat Tours: Experience Fogo Island's stunning coastline and rugged shores by embarking on a kayaking excursion or joining a boat tour. Paddle through pristine waters, discover hidden coves, and marvel at the breathtaking scenery.
Berry Picking: Depending on the season, visitors can engage in the traditional activity of berry picking. Fogo Island is known for its abundance of wild berries, including blueberries, partridgeberries, and bakeapples. Delight in the flavors of the land as you gather these natural treasures.

Fogo Island offers a captivating blend of natural wonders, contemporary architecture, and cultural experiences in the heart of Newfoundland and Labrador's Central region.

Whether you choose to stay at a renowned inn, savor local cuisine, explore art galleries, or engage in outdoor activities, Fogo Island provides a truly unique and unforgettable experience for visitors seeking to immerse themselves in the beauty and authenticity of this remarkable island.

Grand Falls-Windsor

Grand Falls-Windsor is a vibrant town located in the Central region of Newfoundland and Labrador. With its picturesque setting, rich history, and abundance of outdoor activities, it offers a variety of experiences for visitors.

Here are some highlights of places to stay, eat, see, and outdoor activities in Grand Falls-Windsor:

Places to Stay:

Mount Peyton Hotel: This centrally located hotel offers comfortable rooms with modern amenities. Enjoy scenic views of the Exploits River and convenient access to shopping areas and local attractions.

Riverfront Chalets: For a cozy and picturesque stay, consider the Riverfront Chalets. These charming chalets offer self-catering accommodations with beautiful views of the Exploits River.

Places to Eat:

Corduroy Brook Nature Centre & Café: Indulge in delicious meals at the Corduroy Brook Nature Centre & Café. Enjoy a menu featuring locally sourced ingredients, including fresh seafood, homemade soups, sandwiches, and baked goods.

Exploits Valley Salmon Festival: If you happen to visit during the Exploits Valley Salmon Festival, you can enjoy a variety of food vendors offering tasty treats, including traditional Newfoundland dishes and festival favorites.

Places to Visit:

Salmonid Interpretation Centre: Explore the Salmonid Interpretation Centre, which provides educational exhibits on the life cycle of salmon and their importance to the region.
You can observe live salmon in the onsite fishway and learn about the efforts to conserve their populations.

Mary March Provincial Museum: Visit the Mary March Provincial Museum, which showcases the history and culture of Grand Falls-Windsor and the surrounding area. Explore exhibits featuring artifacts, photographs, and stories that highlight the town's heritage.

Outdoor Activities:

Exploits River: Experience the natural beauty of the Exploits River, which offers opportunities for boating, canoeing, and kayaking. Enjoy a peaceful paddle along the river's calm waters and take in the scenic surroundings.

Corduroy Brook Nature Trail: Take a leisurely stroll along the Corduroy Brook Nature Trail, which winds through a picturesque forested area. Enjoy the tranquility of the trail and keep an eye out for local wildlife.

Golfing: Golf enthusiasts can tee off at the Grand Falls Golf Club, a picturesque 18-hole golf course that offers beautiful views of the Exploits River and challenging fairways.

Grand Falls-Windsor offers a mix of natural beauty, cultural experiences, and outdoor activities in the heart of Newfoundland and Labrador's Central region.

Whether you choose to stay in a comfortable hotel, savor local cuisine, explore museums and historic sites, or engage in outdoor adventures, Grand Falls-Windsor provides a memorable and enjoyable experience for visitors seeking to immerse themselves in the charm of this vibrant town.

Gander

Gander is a vibrant town located in the Central region of Newfoundland and Labrador. Known for its warm hospitality, rich aviation history, and scenic surroundings, Gander offers a range of experiences for visitors.

Here are some highlights of places to stay, eat, see, and outdoor activities in Gander:

Places to Stay:

Hotel Gander: This centrally located hotel offers comfortable accommodations with modern amenities. Enjoy convenient access to shopping areas, restaurants, and local attractions.

Albatross Hotel: Situated near the airport, the Albatross Hotel provides cozy rooms and excellent service. Take advantage of their on-site restaurant and lounge for a convenient dining experience.

Places to Eat:

My Brother's Place: Indulge in homestyle Newfoundland cuisine at My Brother's Place. Enjoy a variety of dishes featuring fresh seafood, hearty stews, and traditional desserts. Don't miss the opportunity to try the famous Jiggs dinner.

Rosie's Restaurant: This family-friendly restaurant offers a diverse menu, including burgers, sandwiches, seafood, and vegetarian options.

Enjoy a casual dining experience with friendly service.

Places to Visit:

Silent Witness Memorial: Visit the Silent Witness Memorial, a tribute to the role Gander played during the September 11 attacks. The memorial honors the passengers and crew members who were diverted to Gander during the crisis.

Thomas Howe Demonstration Forest: Explore the Thomas Howe Demonstration Forest, a scenic nature reserve offering well-maintained trails and interpretive signs. Experience the beauty of Newfoundland's boreal forest and discover local flora and fauna.

Outdoor Activities:

Cobb's Pond Rotary Park: Take a leisurely stroll or enjoy a picnic at Cobb's Pond Rotary Park. This beautiful park offers walking trails, playgrounds, and serene pond views. It's an ideal spot for relaxation and outdoor activities.

Little Harbour Marina: If you enjoy boating or fishing, visit Little Harbour Marina. Rent a boat, cast your line, and explore the picturesque waters of Gander Lake. Enjoy the tranquility of the surroundings and the opportunity to catch various fish species.

Gander Golf Club: Tee off at the Gander Golf Club, a scenic 18-hole golf course nestled in the countryside. Challenge your golf skills while taking in the beauty of the rolling fairways and pristine greens.

Gander provides a warm and welcoming atmosphere, with a range of accommodations, dining options, and outdoor activities to suit various interests.

Whether you choose to stay in a comfortable hotel, sample local cuisine, explore historic landmarks, or engage in outdoor adventures, Gander offers a memorable experience in the heart of Newfoundland and Labrador's Central region.

Terra Nova National Park

Terra Nova National Park is a pristine wilderness located in the Central region of Newfoundland and Labrador. Spanning over 400 square kilometers, it offers a diverse range of ecosystems, stunning landscapes, and outdoor activities.

Here are some highlights of places to stay, eat, see, and outdoor activities in Terra Nova National Park:

Places to Stay:

Newman Sound Campground: Experience the beauty of nature by camping at the Newman Sound Campground. It offers a variety of campsites, including those with electrical hookups. Enjoy the serenity of the park and the convenience of amenities such as washrooms, showers, and a playground.

Terra Nova Resort & Golf Community: If you prefer a more luxurious stay, consider the Terra Nova Resort & Golf Community. This beautiful resort offers comfortable accommodations, a golf course, and access to various outdoor activities.

Places to Eat:

The Wilds at Salmonier River: Located near Terra Nova National Park, The Wilds at Salmonier River offers a restaurant that serves delicious meals featuring locally sourced ingredients. Enjoy a variety of dishes, including seafood, steaks, and vegetarian options.

Clode Sound Motel & Restaurant: Just outside the park, Clode Sound Motel & Restaurant offers a cozy dining experience. Savor home-cooked meals, including traditional Newfoundland dishes such as fish and chips, seafood chowder, and toutons.

Places to Visit:

Visitor Centre: Start your journey at the Visitor Centre, where you can learn about the park's natural and cultural history. Explore exhibits, watch informative videos, and speak with park staff for guidance on the best places to explore within the park.

Ochre Hill Trail: Embark on the Ochre Hill Trail, a scenic hiking trail that offers panoramic views of Clode Sound and the surrounding forests. Keep an eye out for wildlife and enjoy the tranquility of nature.

Sandy Pond: Relax and unwind at Sandy Pond, a beautiful freshwater lake within the park. Enjoy swimming, canoeing, or simply basking in the sun on the sandy beach.

Outdoor Activities:

Hiking: Terra Nova National Park offers a network of well-maintained hiking trails suitable for all levels of experience. From easy strolls to more challenging hikes, you can explore the park's diverse landscapes, including boreal forests, rugged coastlines, and serene ponds.

Boating and Kayaking: Explore the park's waterways by boating or kayaking. Paddle along sheltered bays, explore secluded islands, and experience the tranquility of the park's coastal waters.

Wildlife Watching: Keep an eye out for wildlife while exploring Terra Nova National Park. The park is home to a variety of animals, including moose, beavers, otters, and numerous bird species. Take your time to observe and appreciate the natural beauty that surrounds you.

Terra Nova National Park offers a true escape into nature, with its pristine landscapes, outdoor activities, and opportunities for relaxation.

Whether you choose to camp under the stars, savor local cuisine, explore scenic trails, or engage in water-based adventures, Terra Nova National Park provides a memorable and immersive experience for visitors seeking to connect with the beauty of the natural world in the heart of Newfoundland and Labrador's Central region.

Eastern Region

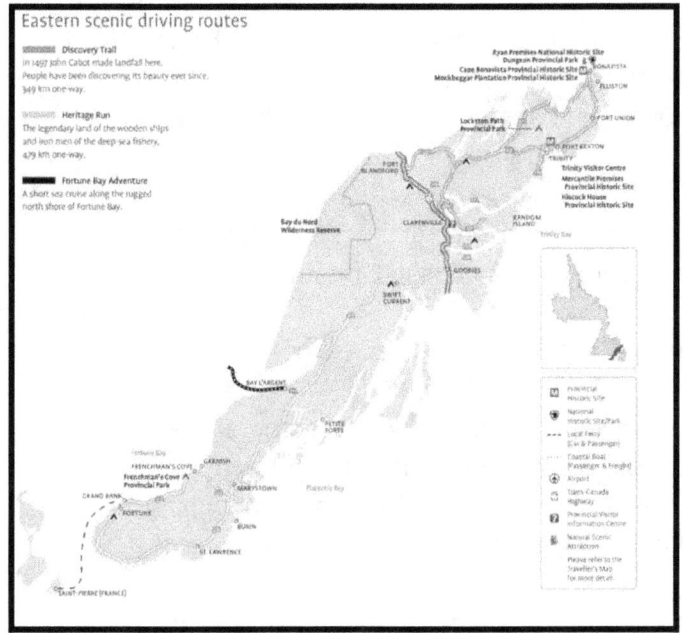

Clarenville

Clarenville is a charming town located on the East Coast of Newfoundland and Labrador. With its picturesque waterfront, scenic trails, and warm community atmosphere, Clarenville offers a range of experiences for visitors.

Here are some highlights of places to stay, eat, see, and outdoor activities in Clarenville:

Places to Stay:

St. Jude Hotel: This centrally located hotel offers comfortable accommodations with modern amenities. Enjoy convenient access to shopping areas, restaurants, and local attractions.

Clarenville Inn: Situated near the waterfront, the Clarenville Inn provides cozy rooms and excellent service. Take advantage of their on-site restaurant and lounge for a convenient dining experience.

Places to Eat:

Classic Café East: Indulge in delicious meals at Classic Café East. This cozy café offers a variety of dishes, including homemade soups, sandwiches, wraps, and baked goods. Enjoy their friendly atmosphere and daily specials.

O'Brien's Music Lounge & Eatery: Located in a historic building, O'Brien's offers a unique dining experience. Enjoy a diverse menu that includes pub-style fare, seafood dishes, and live entertainment.

Places to Visit:

Elizabeth Swan Memorial Park: Explore the Elizabeth Swan Memorial Park, a picturesque waterfront park offering walking trails, picnic areas, and stunning views of Random Sound. Take a leisurely stroll along the boardwalk and enjoy the tranquility of the surroundings.

Random Passage Site: Visit the Random Passage Site, a living history museum that recreates a 19th-century fishing village. Experience the lifestyle and traditions of early settlers through interactive exhibits, demonstrations, and guided tours.

Outdoor Activities:

Clarenville Trailway: Take a walk or bike ride along the Clarenville Trailway, a scenic trail that follows the former rail bed. Enjoy beautiful views of the surrounding countryside and connect with nature as you explore the trail.

White Hills Ski Resort: If you're visiting during the winter months, head to White Hills Ski Resort, located just outside of Clarenville. Enjoy downhill skiing, snowboarding, and tubing on the slopes, or try cross-country skiing and snowshoeing on the nearby trails.

Terra Nova National Park: Explore the nearby Terra Nova National Park, which offers a range of outdoor activities such as hiking, boating, and wildlife watching. Take in the breathtaking coastal scenery, explore the park's trails, and immerse yourself in nature.

Clarenville provides a delightful blend of natural beauty, cultural experiences, and outdoor activities on the East Coast of Newfoundland and Labrador.

Whether you choose to stay in a comfortable hotel, sample local cuisine, explore scenic parks, or engage in outdoor adventures, Clarenville offers a memorable and enjoyable experience for visitors seeking to immerse themselves in the charm and tranquility of this coastal town.

Bonavista

Bonavista is a historic town located on the East Coast of Newfoundland and Labrador. With its rich maritime heritage, stunning coastal scenery, and abundance of outdoor activities, Bonavista offers a range of experiences for visitors.

Here are some highlights of places to stay, eat, see, and outdoor activities in Bonavista:

Places to Stay:

Harbour Quarters Inn: This charming inn offers comfortable accommodations with a waterfront location. Enjoy cozy rooms, friendly service, and beautiful views of the harbor.

Lancaster Inn: Situated in a historic building, the Lancaster Inn provides a unique stay with modern amenities. Experience the charm of this boutique inn and its convenient location near local attractions.

Places to Eat:

The Boreal Diner: Indulge in delicious meals at The Boreal Diner, a cozy restaurant that offers a fusion of international and local cuisine. Enjoy their farm-to-table approach and try dishes featuring fresh seafood, locally sourced ingredients, and homemade desserts.

The Twine Loft: Located in a restored fishing room, The Twine Loft offers a fine dining experience with a focus on local flavors and seasonal ingredients. Enjoy exquisite dishes, an extensive wine list, and panoramic views of the coastline.

Places to Visit:

Ryan Premises National Historic Site: Visit the Ryan Premises National Historic Site, a restored merchant's premises that offers a glimpse into Bonavista's fishing and trading history.

Explore exhibits, artifacts, and interactive displays that showcase the town's maritime heritage.

Cape Bonavista Lighthouse: Discover the iconic Cape Bonavista Lighthouse, a historic structure that dates back to the early 19th century. Climb to the top for panoramic views of the rugged coastline and keep an eye out for whales and icebergs during the season.

Outdoor Activities:

Cape Bonavista: Explore the scenic Cape Bonavista, which offers breathtaking views of the North Atlantic Ocean. Take a leisurely walk along the coastal trails, breathe in the fresh sea air, and enjoy the beauty of the rugged cliffs and picturesque coves.

Elliston Puffin Viewing Site: Head to the nearby town of Elliston, known as the "Root Cellar Capital of the World," and visit the Elliston Puffin Viewing Site. Witness thousands of puffins nesting on the cliffs, along with other seabirds such as kittiwakes and murres.

Dungeon Provincial Park: Experience the unique geological formations at Dungeon Provincial Park. Marvel at the towering sea stacks, sea caves, and natural arches carved by the powerful ocean waves.

Take a scenic hike along the coastal trail and appreciate the raw beauty of the area.

Bonavista offers a captivating blend of history, natural beauty, and outdoor adventures on the East Coast of Newfoundland and Labrador.

Whether you choose to stay in a cozy inn, savor local cuisine, explore historic sites, or immerse yourself in the rugged coastal landscapes, Bonavista provides a memorable and enriching experience for visitors seeking to connect with the region's heritage and natural wonders.

Trinity

Trinity is a picturesque town located on the East Coast of Newfoundland and Labrador. Known for its well-preserved historic charm and stunning coastal scenery, Trinity offers a unique blend of cultural experiences and outdoor adventures.

Here are some highlights of places to stay, eat, see, and outdoor activities in Trinity:

Places to Stay:

Artisan Inn: This charming inn offers a variety of accommodations, including cozy rooms and self-catering vacation homes. Enjoy the warm hospitality, comfortable amenities, and scenic views of Trinity Harbour.

Campbell House: Experience a cozy bed and breakfast stay at Campbell House, a historic property with beautifully appointed rooms. Enjoy the peaceful surroundings and the personalized service of the hosts.

Places to Eat:

Trinity Mercantile: Indulge in delicious meals at Trinity Mercantile, a cozy café and bakery that serves homemade treats, sandwiches, soups, and fresh seafood dishes. Enjoy their warm atmosphere and browse through their selection of local products.

The Twine Loft: Located at the Artisan Inn, The Twine Loft offers a fine dining experience with a focus on locally sourced ingredients. Enjoy innovative dishes and a variety of culinary delights while enjoying breathtaking views of the harbor.

Places to Visit:

Rising Tide Theatre: Immerse yourself in the vibrant local arts scene by attending a performance at Rising Tide Theatre. This professional theatre company showcases Newfoundland and Labrador's cultural heritage through live performances and storytelling.

Trinity Historical Society: Visit the Trinity Historical Society, which preserves and promotes the town's rich history. Explore exhibits and displays that highlight Trinity's role as a significant fishing and trading community in the past.

Outdoor Activities:

Skerwink Trail: Embark on the Skerwink Trail, a scenic coastal hike that offers breathtaking views of rugged cliffs, sea stacks, and picturesque coves. This 5.3-kilometer trail takes you through diverse landscapes and provides opportunities for birdwatching and photography.

Sea Kayaking: Explore Trinity's stunning coastline by sea kayak. Paddle along the rugged shores, explore hidden coves, and keep an eye out for marine wildlife such as whales, seals, and seabirds.

Boat Tours: Take a boat tour to explore the Trinity Bight and surrounding areas. Enjoy the scenic beauty of the coastline, visit nearby islands, and learn about the region's history and ecology from knowledgeable guides.

Trinity offers a unique blend of history, natural beauty, and cultural experiences on the East Coast of Newfoundland and Labrador.

Whether you choose to stay in a cozy inn, savor local cuisine, explore historic sites, or immerse yourself in the breathtaking landscapes, Trinity provides a memorable and enriching experience for visitors seeking to connect with the town's heritage and the beauty of the surrounding coastal region.

Port Rexton

Port Rexton is a charming coastal community located on the East Coast of Newfoundland and Labrador. Known for its stunning landscapes, vibrant arts scene, and outdoor activities, Port Rexton offers a range of experiences for visitors.

Here are some highlights of places to stay, eat, see, and outdoor activities in Port Rexton:

Places to Stay:

Fishers' Loft Inn: This historic inn offers comfortable accommodations with a rustic charm. Enjoy cozy rooms, beautiful gardens, and views of Trinity Bay. The inn also features an on-site restaurant serving delicious meals made with locally sourced ingredients.

Skerwink Hostel: For budget-friendly accommodation, consider the Skerwink Hostel. This cozy and welcoming hostel provides shared and private rooms, communal spaces, and a friendly atmosphere. It is located near the renowned Skerwink Trail.

Places to Eat:

Port Rexton Brewing Co.: Visit the Port Rexton Brewing Co., a popular local craft brewery that also features a taproom and kitchen. Enjoy their selection of handcrafted beers and delicious pub-style food made with locally sourced ingredients.

Two Whales Coffee Shop: Experience the cozy ambiance of the Two Whales Coffee Shop, known for its delicious coffee, homemade baked goods, and light meals. This community-focused café also hosts art exhibitions and live performances.

Places to Visit:

Skerwink Trail: Explore the famous Skerwink Trail, a 5.3-kilometer loop trail that offers breathtaking coastal views, rugged cliffs, and picturesque coves. Experience the natural beauty of the area, including opportunities for birdwatching and spotting marine wildlife.

Port Rexton Historic Fishing Village: Take a stroll through the Port Rexton Historic Fishing Village and immerse yourself in the town's maritime heritage. Explore the preserved fishing stages, boat sheds, and other historic structures that tell the story of the area's fishing industry.

Outdoor Activities:

Sea Kayaking: Experience the stunning coastline of Port Rexton by sea kayak. Take a guided tour and paddle along the rugged shores, exploring hidden coves, sea caves, and scenic islands. Enjoy the serenity of the water and the opportunity to spot wildlife such as whales, seals, and seabirds.
Coastal Hiking:

In addition to the Skerwink Trail, there are other nearby hiking trails in the area, including the Fox Island Trail and the Gun Hill Trail. These trails offer opportunities to immerse yourself in nature, enjoy panoramic views, and witness the rugged beauty of the coastline.

Boat Tours: Join a boat tour from Port Rexton to explore the surrounding waters. Take in the scenic beauty of the coastline, visit nearby islands, and learn about the area's rich marine ecosystem and history.

Port Rexton offers a delightful combination of natural beauty, cultural experiences, and outdoor adventures on the East Coast of Newfoundland and Labrador. Whether you choose to stay in a cozy inn, sample local cuisine, explore the scenic trails, or engage in water-based activities, Port Rexton provides a memorable and enriching experience for visitors seeking to connect with the coastal charm and natural wonders of the region.

Elliston

Elliston is a picturesque coastal town located on the East Coast of Newfoundland and Labrador. Known as the "Root Cellar Capital of the World," Elliston offers a unique blend of natural beauty, cultural heritage, and outdoor activities.

Here are some highlights of places to stay, eat, see, and outdoor activities in Elliston:

Places to Stay:

Seaview Suites: Enjoy comfortable accommodations with stunning ocean views at Seaview Suites. These well-appointed suites provide a cozy and relaxing atmosphere, allowing you to unwind after a day of exploration.

Vacation Rentals: Elliston offers a range of vacation rental properties, including cottages and cabins. These self-catering accommodations allow you to enjoy a home away from home experience while immersing yourself in the town's coastal charm.

Places to Eat:

The Rugged Beauty Boat Tours: Embark on a scenic boat tour with The Rugged Beauty Boat Tours, where you can not only explore the beautiful coastline but also enjoy a delicious meal on board. Feast on fresh seafood, including lobster, crab, and mussels, while taking in the breathtaking views.

Anita's Cafe: Treat yourself to a delightful meal at Anita's Cafe, known for its homestyle cooking and warm hospitality. Enjoy traditional Newfoundland dishes, sandwiches, soups, and freshly baked goods in a cozy and inviting atmosphere.

Places to Visit:

Elliston Root Cellars: Explore the fascinating network of root cellars in Elliston. These traditional structures were used to store root vegetables and other food items. Take a self-guided tour and learn about the town's cultural heritage while admiring the unique architecture.

Elliston Puffin Viewing Site: Witness one of Newfoundland and Labrador's most beloved seabirds, the Atlantic puffin, at the Elliston Puffin Viewing Site. Get a close-up view of these adorable birds as they nest on the cliffs, along with other seabirds such as kittiwakes and murres.

Outdoor Activities:

Coastal Walks: Take a leisurely stroll along the rugged coastline of Elliston and enjoy the breathtaking views of the Atlantic Ocean. Explore the picturesque beaches, sea stacks, and rocky cliffs as you immerse yourself in the natural beauty of the area.

Hiking Trails: Elliston is surrounded by scenic hiking trails that offer opportunities to explore the region's diverse landscapes. The Maberly to Little Catalina Trail and the White Rock Trail are popular options for hikers of all skill levels.

Whale Watching: Join a whale watching tour from Elliston and venture into the Atlantic Ocean to spot magnificent marine creatures. Keep an eye out for humpback whales, fin whales, minke whales, and dolphins as they swim and play in their natural habitat.

Elliston provides a captivating blend of natural wonders, cultural heritage, and outdoor adventures on the East Coast of Newfoundland and Labrador.

Whether you choose to stay in a comfortable suite, sample local cuisine, explore the unique root cellars, or engage in outdoor activities, Elliston offers a memorable and enriching experience for visitors seeking to connect with the coastal charm and natural treasures of the region.

Dildo

Dildo is a charming community located on the East Coast of Newfoundland and Labrador. With its scenic coastal beauty, rich history, and recreational opportunities, Dildo offers visitors a unique and enjoyable experience.

Here are some highlights of places to stay, eat, see, and outdoor activities in Dildo:

Places to Stay:

George House Heritage Bed and Breakfast: Experience a cozy stay at the George House Heritage Bed and Breakfast. This beautifully restored heritage property offers comfortable rooms with a touch of old-world charm. Enjoy warm hospitality and a delicious homemade breakfast.

Dildo Boathouse Inn: Nestled along the waterfront, the Dildo Boathouse Inn provides comfortable accommodations with picturesque views. This boutique inn offers cozy rooms, a restaurant, and a lovely deck where you can relax and enjoy the scenic surroundings.

Places to Eat:

Dildo Dory Grill: Indulge in delicious meals at the Dildo Dory Grill, a waterfront restaurant that specializes in seafood dishes. Enjoy fresh catches of the day, lobster, scallops, and other local favorites. The restaurant also offers stunning views of the harbor.

The Dildo Brewery and Museum: Visit The Dildo Brewery and Museum, a unique establishment that combines a microbrewery, restaurant, and museum. Sample their craft beers, enjoy a tasty meal, and learn about the history and brewing process of Dildo Brewing Co.

Places to Visit:

Dildo Interpretation Centre and Walking Trail: Explore the Dildo Interpretation Centre and learn about the history and heritage of the area. Discover artifacts, exhibits, and displays that showcase the community's maritime past. Take a leisurely walk along the nearby trail, which offers beautiful views of the harbor.

Dildo Island: Take a boat tour to Dildo Island and enjoy the scenic beauty of this small island located just off the coast. Admire the rugged coastline, observe seabirds, and learn about the island's history.

Outdoor Activities:

Kayaking: Experience the stunning coastal scenery of Dildo by going on a kayaking adventure. Paddle along the shoreline, explore hidden coves, and appreciate the natural beauty of the area.

Whale Watching: Join a whale watching tour from Dildo and venture out into the Atlantic Ocean to spot magnificent marine creatures. Keep an eye out for humpback whales, minke whales, and other species as they swim and play in their natural habitat.

Hiking and Nature Trails: Discover the beauty of the surrounding landscapes by exploring the hiking and nature trails near Dildo. Enjoy scenic walks, breathe in the fresh air, and immerse yourself in the tranquility of nature.

Dildo offers a delightful mix of coastal charm, history, and outdoor activities on the East Coast of Newfoundland and Labrador.

Whether you choose to stay in a cozy bed and breakfast, sample local cuisine, explore the interpretation center, or engage in outdoor adventures, Dildo provides a memorable and enjoyable experience for visitors seeking relaxation, natural beauty, and a touch of maritime history.

Avalon Peninsula

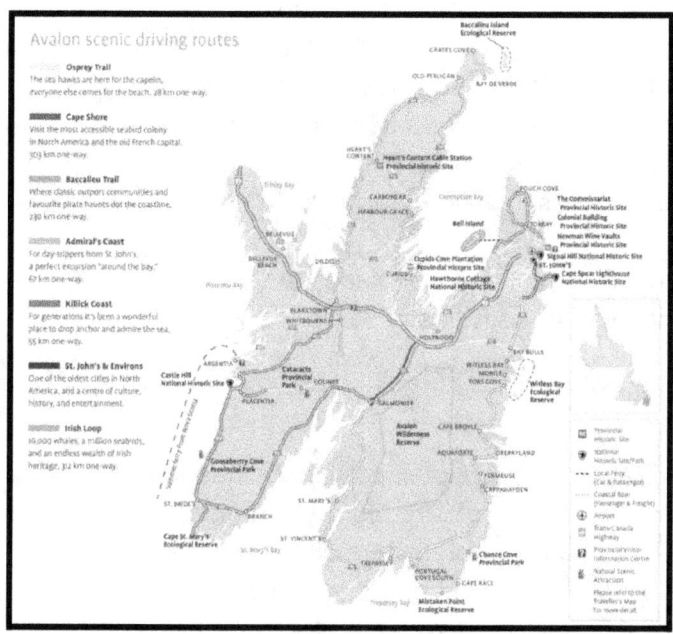

St. John's

St. John's, located on the Avalon Peninsula, is the vibrant capital city of Newfoundland and Labrador. Known for its colorful row houses, rich history, and stunning coastal landscapes, St. John's offers a wide range of attractions, dining options, and outdoor activities.

Here are some highlights of places to stay, eat, see, and outdoor activities in St. John's:

Places to Stay:

The Murray Premises Hotel: Stay in the heart of downtown St. John's at The Murray Premises Hotel. This boutique hotel offers comfortable rooms with a blend of historic charm and modern amenities. Enjoy the convenient location within walking distance of popular attractions, restaurants, and shops.

Sheraton Hotel Newfoundland: Experience luxury accommodations at the Sheraton Hotel Newfoundland. Located on the harborfront, this upscale hotel features spacious rooms, excellent dining options, and stunning views of the surrounding area.

Places to Eat:

Raymonds: Indulge in an exquisite dining experience at Raymonds, a renowned restaurant that showcases the best of Newfoundland cuisine.

Enjoy creative dishes crafted with locally sourced ingredients and an extensive wine list in an elegant setting.

Mallard Cottage: Experience rustic charm and traditional Newfoundland fare at Mallard Cottage. Located in a restored historic cottage, this restaurant offers a menu inspired by local ingredients and traditional cooking methods.

Places to Visit:

Signal Hill: Visit Signal Hill, an iconic landmark overlooking St. John's Harbor. Explore the historic site, including the Cabot Tower, which offers panoramic views of the city and the coastline. Take a leisurely hike along the trails and immerse yourself in the natural beauty of the area.

The Rooms: Discover the art, history, and culture of Newfoundland and Labrador at The Rooms. This striking cultural center houses a museum, art gallery, and archives, showcasing exhibits that highlight the province's heritage and artistic talent.

Outdoor Activities:

East Coast Trail: Embark on a section of the East Coast Trail, a scenic coastal trail system that stretches along the Avalon Peninsula. Enjoy breathtaking views, rugged cliffs, and charming fishing communities as you hike through diverse landscapes.

Cape Spear: Visit Cape Spear, the easternmost point in North America. Explore the historic lighthouse, walk along the coastal trails, and witness the power of the Atlantic Ocean as it crashes against the rugged cliffs.

Whale Watching Tours: Join a whale watching tour from St. John's and venture out into the ocean to spot majestic whales, including humpbacks, orcas, and minke whales. Marvel at their impressive displays as they breach and surface near your boat.

St. John's offers a captivating mix of history, culture, culinary delights, and outdoor adventures on the Avalon Peninsula.

Whether you choose to stay in a boutique hotel, savor local cuisine, explore historic sites, or engage in outdoor activities, St. John's provides a memorable and vibrant experience for visitors seeking to immerse themselves in the charm and natural wonders of Newfoundland and Labrador.

Cape Spear

Cape Spear is a stunning coastal area located on the Avalon Peninsula, just a short drive from St. John's. As the easternmost point in North America, Cape Spear offers breathtaking views, historical significance, and outdoor activities.

Here are some highlights of places to stay, eat, see, and outdoor activities in Cape Spear:

Places to Stay:

St. John's Downtown Hotels: Cape Spear is conveniently located near St. John's, where you'll find a variety of hotels and accommodations. Stay in the downtown area to enjoy easy access to Cape Spear and other attractions on the Avalon Peninsula.

Places to Eat:

Ches's Famous Fish & Chips: Head to Ches's Famous Fish & Chips in St. John's to savor a classic Newfoundland meal. Enjoy crispy fish and chips, tasty seafood chowder, and other local favorites in a casual dining atmosphere.

Bernard Stanley's Smokehouse: If you're craving delicious smoked salmon, visit Bernard Stanley's Smokehouse. Located in St. John's, this smokehouse offers a range of smoked fish products, including salmon, trout, and mackerel.

Places to Visit:

Cape Spear Lighthouse: Visit the Cape Spear Lighthouse, the oldest surviving lighthouse in Newfoundland and Labrador. Explore the historical exhibits, climb to the top of the lighthouse, and enjoy panoramic views of the rugged coastline.

Cape Spear National Historic Site: Take a stroll through the Cape Spear National Historic Site and discover military fortifications that date back to World War II. Learn about the area's role in defending the coast and explore the interpretive displays.

Outdoor Activities:

Coastal Walks and Hiking Trails: Enjoy the natural beauty of Cape Spear by taking a leisurely coastal walk or hiking along the trails. The East Coast Trail passes through Cape Spear, offering scenic views of the rugged cliffs, ocean vistas, and wildlife sightings.

Whale Watching: Join a whale watching tour departing from St. John's and sail into the Atlantic Ocean to spot majestic marine life. Keep an eye out for humpback whales, fin whales, dolphins, and seabirds as they grace the waters around Cape Spear.

Picnicking and Scenic Photography: Bring a picnic lunch and find a scenic spot along the rugged coastline to enjoy a meal with breathtaking views. Cape Spear provides an ideal setting for capturing stunning photographs of the dramatic landscapes and the crashing waves.

Cape Spear offers a unique combination of historical significance, natural beauty, and outdoor activities on the Avalon Peninsula.

Whether you choose to explore the historic lighthouse, savor local cuisine, hike along the coastline, or embark on a whale watching adventure, Cape Spear provides an unforgettable experience for visitors seeking to immerse themselves in the rugged charm of Newfoundland and Labrador.

Quidi Vidi

Quidi Vidi is a picturesque village located on the Avalon Peninsula, just a short distance from downtown St. John's. Known for its scenic beauty, charming fishing heritage, and vibrant community, Quidi Vidi offers a delightful mix of places to stay, eat, see, and outdoor activities.

Here are some highlights:

Places to Stay:

Quidi Vidi Village Plantation: Immerse yourself in the local culture by staying at the Quidi Vidi Village Plantation. This unique accommodation offers artist studios, workshops, and a bed and breakfast. Experience the creative spirit of Quidi Vidi and enjoy the cozy and artistic atmosphere.

Downtown St. John's Hotels: Quidi Vidi is conveniently located near downtown St. John's, where you'll find a variety of hotels and accommodations. Stay in the city center to enjoy easy access to Quidi Vidi and other attractions on the Avalon Peninsula.

Places to Eat:

Quidi Vidi Brewery & Tap Room: Indulge in craft beer and delicious pub fare at the Quidi Vidi Brewery & Tap Room. Sample a wide selection of locally brewed beers while enjoying views of the historic fishing village. The tap room also offers a menu featuring tasty bites and pub-style dishes.

Mallard Cottage: Located nearby in Quidi Vidi Village, Mallard Cottage is a renowned restaurant known for its farm-to-table dining experience. Enjoy seasonal, locally sourced ingredients transformed into creative and delicious dishes.

Places to Visit:

Quidi Vidi Gut: Take a stroll along the picturesque Quidi Vidi Gut, a narrow inlet that separates Quidi Vidi Village from the rest of St. John's. Admire the colorful fishing stages, historic houses, and fishing boats, all set against a backdrop of rugged cliffs and rolling hills.

Quidi Vidi Battery Provincial Historic Site: Explore the Quidi Vidi Battery, a historic site that dates back to the 18th century. Learn about its significance in defending the harbor and enjoy panoramic views of Quidi Vidi Village, the Gut, and the surrounding coastline.

Outdoor Activities:

Quidi Vidi Lake: Enjoy a leisurely stroll around Quidi Vidi Lake, a serene body of water surrounded by picturesque landscapes. The lake is a popular spot for walking, jogging, picnicking, and birdwatching.

East Coast Trail: Accessible from Quidi Vidi, the East Coast Trail offers scenic hiking trails that wind along the rugged coastline. Explore the picturesque cliffs, secluded coves, and panoramic vistas that make this trail system a favorite among outdoor enthusiasts.

Quidi Vidi offers a tranquil escape with its scenic beauty, rich history, and culinary delights on the Avalon Peninsula.

Whether you choose to stay in a unique artistic accommodation, indulge in local cuisine, explore the village's charming sites, or engage in outdoor activities, Quidi Vidi provides a memorable and picturesque experience for visitors seeking relaxation, natural beauty, and cultural immersion in Newfoundland and Labrador.

Petty Harbour

Petty Harbour, located on the Avalon Peninsula, is a charming fishing village known for its picturesque harbor, colorful houses, and rich maritime history. With its tranquil atmosphere and natural beauty, Petty Harbour offers a range of places to stay, eat, see, and outdoor activities.

Here are some highlights:

Places to Stay:

The Miniature Cottage: Experience a unique stay at The Miniature Cottage, a cozy vacation rental located in the heart of Petty Harbour. This charming cottage offers comfortable accommodations with stunning views of the harbor and easy access to the village's attractions.

Nearby Hotels: Petty Harbour is conveniently located near St. John's, where you'll find a variety of hotels and accommodations. Stay in St. John's to enjoy the amenities of the city while exploring Petty Harbour and the surrounding area.

Places to Eat:

Chafe's Landing: Enjoy a delicious seafood meal at Chafe's Landing, a waterfront restaurant in Petty Harbour. Indulge in fresh local fish, lobster, crab, and other seafood specialties while taking in the scenic views of the harbor.

The Watershed Coffee Shop: Start your day with a cup of freshly brewed coffee or enjoy a light meal at The Watershed Coffee Shop. This cozy café offers a relaxed atmosphere and a selection of baked goods, sandwiches, and beverages.

Places to Visit:

Petty Harbour Fishermen's Museum: Visit the Petty Harbour Fishermen's Museum and learn about the village's rich fishing heritage. Explore exhibits that showcase the traditional fishing methods, tools, and artifacts, and gain insights into the daily life of the local fishermen.

Petty Harbour Mini Aquarium: Discover the wonders of the local marine life at the Petty Harbour Mini Aquarium. This educational facility showcases a variety of fish, invertebrates, and other marine species found in the waters around Newfoundland and Labrador.

Outdoor Activities:

Whale Watching: Embark on a whale watching tour from Petty Harbour and experience the thrill of spotting majestic whales in their natural habitat. Keep an eye out for humpback whales, minke whales, and dolphins as they swim and play in the waters off the coast.

Coastal Walks and Hiking: Enjoy the scenic beauty of Petty Harbour and the surrounding area by taking a leisurely coastal walk or exploring nearby

hiking trails. Experience stunning views of the rugged coastline, cliffs, and panoramic vistas.
Fishing and Boating: Petty Harbour is a great place for fishing enthusiasts. Charter a boat and try your hand at catching cod, mackerel, or other local fish species.

Alternatively, you can rent a kayak or canoe and explore the calm waters of the harbor.
Petty Harbour offers a peaceful retreat with its coastal charm, maritime history, and outdoor activities on the Avalon Peninsula.

Whether you choose to stay in a cozy cottage, indulge in fresh seafood, explore the village's museums, or engage in outdoor adventures, Petty Harbour provides a serene and authentic Newfoundland experience for visitors seeking relaxation, cultural immersion, and natural beauty.

Brigus

Brigus, located on the Avalon Peninsula, is a historic and picturesque town that offers a glimpse into Newfoundland's past. With its well-preserved architecture, scenic harbor, and charming atmosphere, Brigus is a popular destination for visitors seeking a blend of history, natural beauty, and outdoor activities.

Here are some highlights of places to stay, eat, see, and outdoor activities in Brigus:

Places to Stay:

The Baccalieu Trail Bed & Breakfast: Experience warm hospitality and comfortable accommodations at The Baccalieu Trail Bed & Breakfast in Brigus. This charming B&B offers cozy rooms, delicious breakfast, and easy access to the town's attractions.

Nearby Cottages and Vacation Rentals: Brigus and its surrounding area offer a range of cottages and vacation rentals for those seeking a self-catering accommodation option. Enjoy the privacy and flexibility of a cottage while immersing yourself in the town's ambiance.

Places to Eat:

The Country Corner Restaurant: Indulge in homestyle Newfoundland cuisine at The Country Corner Restaurant. This cozy eatery serves up traditional dishes such as fish and chips, seafood chowder, and toutons (fried dough). Don't miss out on their delicious homemade pies and desserts.

The Brigus Blueberry Festival: If you visit Brigus during the annual Brigus Blueberry Festival, you'll have the chance to enjoy a variety of local food vendors and culinary delights. This festival celebrates the town's blueberry harvest and features live music, entertainment, and family-friendly activities.

Places to Visit:

Hawthorne Cottage National Historic Site: Explore Hawthorne Cottage, the former home of Arctic explorer Captain Robert Bartlett. This national historic site provides insight into Bartlett's life and achievements and offers beautiful views of the harbor.

Brigus Tunnel: Take a stroll along the Brigus Tunnel, a unique underground passageway that was built in the 19th century to transport water from a nearby pond to the town. The tunnel is an intriguing piece of engineering history and is open for visitors to explore.

Outdoor Activities:

Brigus Boardwalk: Enjoy a leisurely walk along the Brigus Boardwalk, which offers stunning views of the harbor and surrounding landscapes. Take in the fresh sea air and admire the colorful houses and boats that line the waterfront.

Coastal Explorations: Explore the rugged coastline and nearby trails for scenic walks and hikes. The area surrounding Brigus offers opportunities to discover beautiful landscapes, picturesque coves, and panoramic views of the Atlantic Ocean.

Fishing and Boating: Experience the traditional Newfoundland pastime of fishing by joining a fishing charter or renting a boat. Brigus and its surrounding waters offer excellent fishing opportunities, including cod fishing and recreational boating.

Brigus captures the essence of Newfoundland's history and natural beauty, offering a tranquil escape on the Avalon Peninsula.

Whether you choose to stay in a cozy bed and breakfast, savor local cuisine, explore the town's historic sites, or engage in outdoor adventures, Brigus provides a charming and immersive experience for visitors seeking a glimpse into the province's past and a chance to connect with nature.

Cupids

Cupids, located on the Avalon Peninsula, holds the distinction of being the oldest continuously settled English colony in Canada. Steeped in history and surrounded by natural beauty, Cupids offers a unique blend of cultural heritage and outdoor activities.

Here are some highlights of places to stay, eat, see, and outdoor activities in Cupids:

Places to Stay:

Cupids Legacy Centre: Immerse yourself in the town's history by staying at the Cupids Legacy Centre. This cultural facility offers accommodations in restored 19th-century buildings, allowing you to experience a blend of modern comfort and historic charm. Learn about the town's early settlement and explore the exhibits and archives within the center.

Places to Eat:

Cupids Haven: Enjoy a meal at Cupids Haven, a quaint restaurant offering a range of traditional Newfoundland dishes. Indulge in seafood specialties, hearty stews, and homemade desserts while taking in the cozy and welcoming atmosphere.

Nearby Cafés and Bakeries: Cupids is surrounded by charming cafés and bakeries where you can grab a quick bite or treat yourself to freshly baked goods and a cup of coffee.

Places to Visit:

Cupids Cove Plantation: Visit the Cupids Cove Plantation, a Parks Canada National Historic Site, which provides a fascinating glimpse into the early English settlement in the region.

Explore the archaeological remains, interpretive exhibits, and reconstructed buildings that showcase the town's history and cultural significance.

Green's Harbour: Take a short drive to Green's Harbour, a neighboring community known for its scenic beauty and stunning coastal views. Enjoy a leisurely walk along the shoreline, take in the peaceful atmosphere, and admire the picturesque landscapes.

Outdoor Activities:

Cupids Cove Soiree: If you visit Cupids during the Cupids Cove Soiree, a summer festival held annually, you can partake in outdoor concerts, traditional Newfoundland music, dancing, and other cultural activities.

Hiking and Nature Trails: Lace up your hiking boots and explore the scenic trails surrounding Cupids. Enjoy peaceful walks through forests, meadows, and along coastal paths, taking in the natural beauty of the Avalon Peninsula.

Sea Kayaking and Boat Tours: Experience the rugged coastline and picturesque bays of Cupids through sea kayaking or boat tours. Enjoy the opportunity to spot wildlife, explore hidden coves, and learn about the area's natural history and geology.

Cupids offers a captivating blend of history, culture, and outdoor exploration on the Avalon Peninsula.

Whether you choose to stay in a historic accommodation, sample local cuisine, visit the town's heritage sites, or engage in outdoor adventures, Cupids provides a unique and enriching experience for visitors seeking to delve into Newfoundland's past and enjoy its natural surroundings.

Bay Bulls

Bay Bulls, located on the Avalon Peninsula, is a scenic coastal community known for its stunning views, abundant wildlife, and rich cultural heritage. With its proximity to the Witless Bay Ecological Reserve and a range of outdoor activities, Bay Bulls is a popular destination for nature enthusiasts and those seeking a tranquil getaway.

Here are some highlights of places to stay, eat, see, and outdoor activities in Bay Bulls:

Places to Stay:

The Captain's Quarters: Stay at The Captain's Quarters, a charming bed and breakfast located in the heart of Bay Bulls. This cozy accommodation offers comfortable rooms, warm hospitality, and a convenient location close to the town's attractions and outdoor activities.

Vacation Rentals: Bay Bulls and its surrounding area offer a variety of vacation rentals, including cottages and seaside homes. Renting a vacation property allows you to enjoy privacy and a home-away-from-home experience during your stay.

Places to Eat:

The Sailor's Galley: Dine at The Sailor's Galley, a popular restaurant in Bay Bulls known for its fresh seafood dishes and local specialties. Enjoy delicious fish and chips, seafood chowder, and other maritime favorites while taking in the views of the harbor.

Nearby Cafés and Bakeries: Bay Bulls is home to several charming cafés and bakeries where you can grab a cup of coffee, enjoy homemade pastries, and savor light meals and snacks.

Places to Visit:

Witless Bay Ecological Reserve: Take a boat tour from Bay Bulls to the Witless Bay Ecological Reserve, a protected area renowned for its seabird colonies. Witness the spectacle of thousands of puffins, murres, and other seabirds nesting on the rocky cliffs and explore the rich marine life in the surrounding waters.

Bay Bulls Harbour: Explore the picturesque Bay Bulls Harbour, where colorful fishing boats dot the waterfront. Take a stroll along the wharf, soak in the serene atmosphere, and admire the beautiful coastal views.

Outdoor Activities:

Whale and Puffin Watching: Join a boat tour from Bay Bulls to observe majestic whales and charming puffins up close. Experience the thrill of spotting humpback whales, minke whales, and other marine wildlife as they navigate the waters around the Avalon Peninsula.

Sea Kayaking: Embark on a sea kayaking adventure and paddle along the rugged coastline of Bay Bulls. Enjoy the tranquility of the sea, explore hidden coves, and appreciate the breathtaking scenery while keeping an eye out for marine life.

East Coast Trail: Bay Bulls serves as a gateway to the East Coast Trail, a scenic coastal hiking trail that spans the Avalon Peninsula. Explore sections of the trail near Bay Bulls and immerse yourself in the rugged beauty of Newfoundland's coastal landscapes.

Bay Bulls offers a captivating blend of natural beauty, wildlife encounters, and outdoor adventures on the Avalon Peninsula.

Whether you choose to stay in a cozy bed and breakfast, indulge in fresh seafood, explore the ecological reserve, or engage in outdoor activities, Bay Bulls provides a memorable experience for visitors seeking to connect with nature and appreciate the region's coastal charm.

Ferryland

Ferryland, located on the Avalon Peninsula, is a historic town known for its picturesque coastal landscapes, rich cultural heritage, and the iconic Ferryland Lighthouse. With its scenic beauty, charming atmosphere, and outdoor activities, Ferryland offers a delightful experience for visitors.

Here are some highlights of places to stay, eat, see, and outdoor activities in Ferryland:

Places to Stay:

The Colony of Avalon: Immerse yourself in history by staying at The Colony of Avalon, a historic site that offers comfortable accommodations in restored buildings. Experience the charm of this archaeological site and learn about the town's early settlement while enjoying modern amenities.

Nearby Bed and Breakfasts: Ferryland and its surrounding area offer a variety of bed and breakfasts where you can enjoy a cozy and personalized stay. These accommodations often provide warm hospitality and stunning views of the coastline.

Places to Eat:

The Lighthouse Picnics: Enjoy a unique dining experience at The Lighthouse Picnics, located near the Ferryland Lighthouse. This popular spot offers delicious picnic-style meals featuring local ingredients. Feast on freshly made sandwiches, salads, and desserts while taking in the breathtaking coastal views.

Local Cafés and Restaurants: Explore the town and discover charming cafés and restaurants that serve a variety of dishes, including seafood specialties and traditional Newfoundland cuisine.

Places to Visit:

Ferryland Lighthouse: Visit the iconic Ferryland Lighthouse, perched on the rugged cliffs overlooking the Atlantic Ocean. This historic lighthouse offers stunning panoramic views and is a popular spot for photography enthusiasts. Take a leisurely stroll along the coastline and enjoy the serenity of the surroundings.

Colony of Avalon: Discover the fascinating history of the Colony of Avalon, a 17th-century archaeological site that offers guided tours and exhibits. Explore the remains of the settlement, including the archaeological dig, interpretive center, and reconstructed buildings.

Outdoor Activities:

Coastal Walks: Take advantage of Ferryland's beautiful coastal setting by going for scenic walks along the cliffs and shoreline. Enjoy the fresh sea air, take in the breathtaking views, and keep an eye out for seabirds and marine life.

Hiking Trails: Explore the nearby hiking trails that showcase the natural beauty of the area. The East Coast Trail offers a variety of options, ranging from easy strolls to more challenging hikes, allowing you to immerse yourself in the rugged landscapes and enjoy panoramic vistas.

Whale Watching: Join a whale watching tour and witness the majestic marine mammals that frequent the waters off the Avalon Peninsula. Keep an eye out for humpback whales, minke whales, and other species as they breach and play in the ocean.

Ferryland offers a charming coastal experience, blending history, natural beauty, and outdoor activities on the Avalon Peninsula. Whether you choose to stay in a historic site, savor local cuisine, visit the iconic lighthouse, or engage in outdoor adventures, Ferryland provides a serene and enriching destination for those seeking a peaceful getaway and an appreciation of Newfoundland's cultural and natural heritage.

Labrador

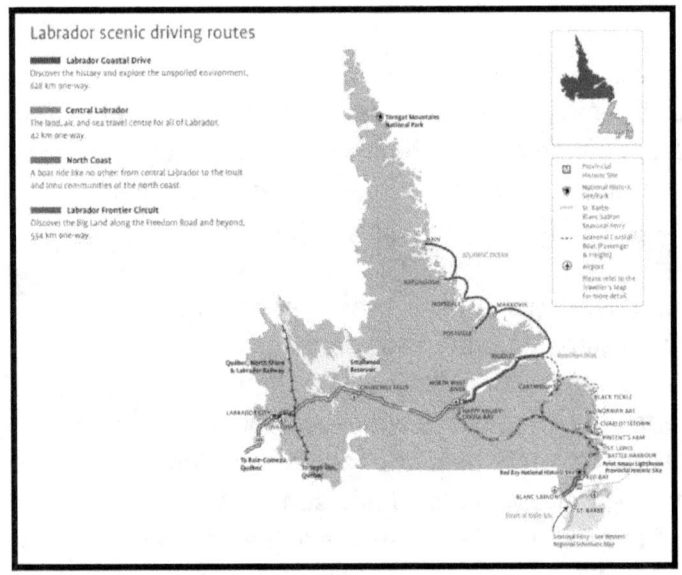

Happy Valley-Goose Bay

Places to Stay: Happy Valley-Goose Bay offers a range of accommodations, including hotels, motels, and bed and breakfasts. Options include the Hotel North Two, Royal Inn and Suites, and numerous cozy bed and breakfasts.

Places to Eat:

Explore local dining options like Trappers' Bakery, which offers delicious pastries and coffee, or The Ivy Restaurant, known for its diverse menu featuring seafood, steaks, and more.

Places to Visit:

Visit the Labrador Interpretation Centre, where you can learn about the local culture, history, and environment. Take a walk along Birch Island Boardwalk to enjoy scenic views of the Churchill River.

Outdoor Activities:

Engage in outdoor activities such as hiking the Birch Island Trail, canoeing or kayaking on the Churchill River, or fishing for trout in nearby lakes and rivers.

Labrador City/Wabush

Places to Stay: Labrador City/Wabush has a range of accommodations, including hotels like the Hotel Labrador and the Wabush Hotel. These establishments provide comfortable rooms and convenient access to amenities.

Places to Eat:

Enjoy dining at local establishments such as Captain's Pub & Eatery or Yummy China Restaurant, offering a variety of cuisine options to satisfy your taste buds.

Places to Visit:

Explore scenic spots like Tanya Lake Park, where you can take leisurely walks, have picnics, and enjoy the tranquility of the surrounding nature.

Outdoor Activities:

Engage in outdoor activities like hiking or mountain biking along the trails of Labrador West, fishing in nearby lakes and rivers, or experiencing winter sports like snowmobiling and cross-country skiing during the snowy season.

Red Bay

Places to Stay:

Red Bay offers various accommodations, including cozy bed and breakfasts and vacation rentals. Consider staying at the Driftwood Inn or nearby campsites for a unique experience.

Places to Eat:

Visit local eateries like the Point Amour Café for delicious meals and refreshing beverages, or enjoy seafood specialties at Dockside Restaurant.

Places to Visit:

Explore the UNESCO World Heritage Site of Red Bay Basque Whaling Station, where you can learn about the area's history and visit the Interpretation Centre and archaeological remains.

Outdoor Activities:

Experience outdoor activities such as hiking the Coastal Trail, which offers breathtaking views of the coastline, or taking boat tours to explore the nearby islands and potentially spot marine wildlife like whales and seabirds.

These communities in Labrador provide a unique blend of natural beauty, cultural heritage, and outdoor adventures. Whether you choose to stay in comfortable accommodations, sample local cuisine, visit historical sites, or engage in outdoor activities, these communities offer a memorable experience that showcases the beauty and charm of Labrador.

Let's Wrap It Up…

Newfoundland and Labrador is a must-visit destination for travelers who are seeking unique outdoor experiences, cultural immersion, and unforgettable adventures.

From exploring the picturesque coastlines to hiking through the rugged landscapes, and indulging in the delicious local cuisine, there is something for everyone in this province. With its rich history, diverse wildlife, and friendly locals, Newfoundland and Labrador is a destination that will leave a lasting impression on any traveler.

Recap of why Newfoundland & Labrador is a great travel destination

Newfoundland & Labrador is a wonderful travel destination that offers a unique blend of natural beauty, rich culture, and exciting adventures. Here are some reasons why it is worth visiting:

1. Stunning natural landscapes: From towering fjords to rugged coastlines, Newfoundland & Labrador is home to some of the most spectacular natural landscapes in the world.

2. Rich cultural heritage: With a history that dates back thousands of years, the region has a rich cultural heritage that is reflected in its traditions, music, food, and art.
3. Exciting outdoor adventures: From hiking and kayaking to snowmobiling and skiing, there are plenty of outdoor activities to keep adventure-seekers entertained.
4. Abundant wildlife: Newfoundland & Labrador is home to a diverse array of wildlife, including whales, moose, caribou, and seabirds.
5. Friendly locals: Visitors to Newfoundland & Labrador are sure to be charmed by the warm hospitality and friendly nature of the locals.

Overall, Newfoundland & Labrador is a destination that has something for everyone, whether you're looking for outdoor adventures, cultural experiences, or simply a chance to relax and soak up the natural beauty of this amazing region.

Final recommendations and tips

Here are some final recommendations and tips for traveling to Newfoundland & Labrador:

1. Plan ahead: Newfoundland & Labrador is a vast and sparsely populated region, so it's important to plan your itinerary in advance to make the most of your time there. Research the top sights and activities, and book any necessary tours or accommodations ahead of time.

2. Be prepared for the weather: The weather in Newfoundland & Labrador can be unpredictable, so be sure to pack for all eventualities. Bring layers, waterproof gear, and sturdy footwear for hiking.
3. Respect the local culture: Newfoundland & Labrador has a rich cultural heritage, and it's important to respect the traditions and customs of the local people. Learn about the history and culture of the region, and be respectful of the environment and wildlife.
4. Try the local food and drink: Newfoundland & Labrador is known for its unique and delicious cuisine, so be sure to try some of the local specialties. Sample fresh seafood, game meat, and traditional dishes like fish and brews.
5. Take advantage of outdoor activities: Newfoundland & Labrador is a paradise for outdoor enthusiasts, with endless opportunities for hiking, kayaking, skiing, and more. Take advantage of the stunning natural scenery and get active.

Here are some useful links to help you plan your trip to Newfoundland & Labrador:
- Newfoundland & Labrador Tourism: https://www.newfoundlandlabrador.com/
- East Coast Trail Association: https://eastcoasttrail.ca/

- Gros Morne National Park: https://www.pc.gc.ca/en/pn-np/nl/grosmorne
- Iceberg Finder: https://www.icebergfinder.com/
- Newfoundland & Labrador Whale Watching: https://www.newfoundlandlabrador.com/things-to-do/whale-watching
- Newfoundland & Labrador Tourism YouTube channel: https://www.youtube.com/user/NewfoundlandLabrador

We hope you have a wonderful trip to Newfoundland & Labrador and enjoy all the natural beauty, culture, and adventure this region has to offer!

Encouragement to visit and experience the province for oneself

Newfoundland & Labrador is a truly unique and unforgettable travel destination. To experience the best of what this province has to offer, here's a detailed list of activities and places to visit:

1. Explore the charming city of St. John's, with its colorful row houses and vibrant nightlife.
2. Hike the stunning East Coast Trail and take in breathtaking coastal views.
3. Visit the UNESCO World Heritage Site of Gros Morne National Park and marvel at its unique geological features.

4. Experience the rich history and culture of Newfoundland & Labrador at The Rooms museum in St. John's.
5. Sample the delicious regional cuisine, including fresh seafood, game meat, and traditional dishes like Jiggs Dinner.
6. Go whale watching and see the majestic humpback whales up close.
7. Spot icebergs along the coast during the spring and early summer.
8. Take part in outdoor adventures like kayaking, canoeing, snowmobiling, and skiing.
9. Visit the remote region of Labrador and discover its fascinating history and culture.
10. Stay in cozy cabins, bed and breakfasts, or luxury accommodations along the way.

Whether you're an adventure-seeker, history buff, or simply seeking a unique and unforgettable travel experience, Newfoundland & Labrador has something for everyone. Don't miss out on this incredible destination **- start planning your trip today!**

Additional Links

St. John's
1. George Street Association - official website of the George Street Association with information on upcoming events, bars, and restaurants: https://georgestreetlive.ca/
2. O'Reilly's Irish Newfoundland Pub - popular pub on George Street known for live music

and traditional Newfoundland cuisine: https://oreillyspub.com/
3. YellowBelly Brewery & Public House - craft brewery and pub located on George Street, with a focus on local ingredients and traditional Newfoundland fare: https://www.yellowbellybrewery.com/
4. The Martini Bar - upscale cocktail bar on George Street known for its extensive cocktail menu and stylish atmosphere: https://www.themartinibar.ca/

Gandar & Come from Away

1. Town of Gander Official Website: https://gandercanada.com/

2. Come From Away Musical Official Website: https://comefromaway.com/

3. Come From Away Virtual Tour: https://www.newfoundlandlabrador.com/plan-and-book/travel-stories/come-from-away-virtual-tour

4. Gander International Airport: https://ganderairport.com/
5. "The Day the World Came to Town: 9/11 in Gander, Newfoundland" (book)

6. https://www.amazon.com/Day-World-Came-Town-Newfoundland/dp/0060559713

L'Anse aux Meadows and Vikings
- Parks Canada - L'Anse aux Meadows National Historic Site: https://www.pc.gc.ca/en/lhn-nhs/nl/meadows

Newfoundland & Labrador Map

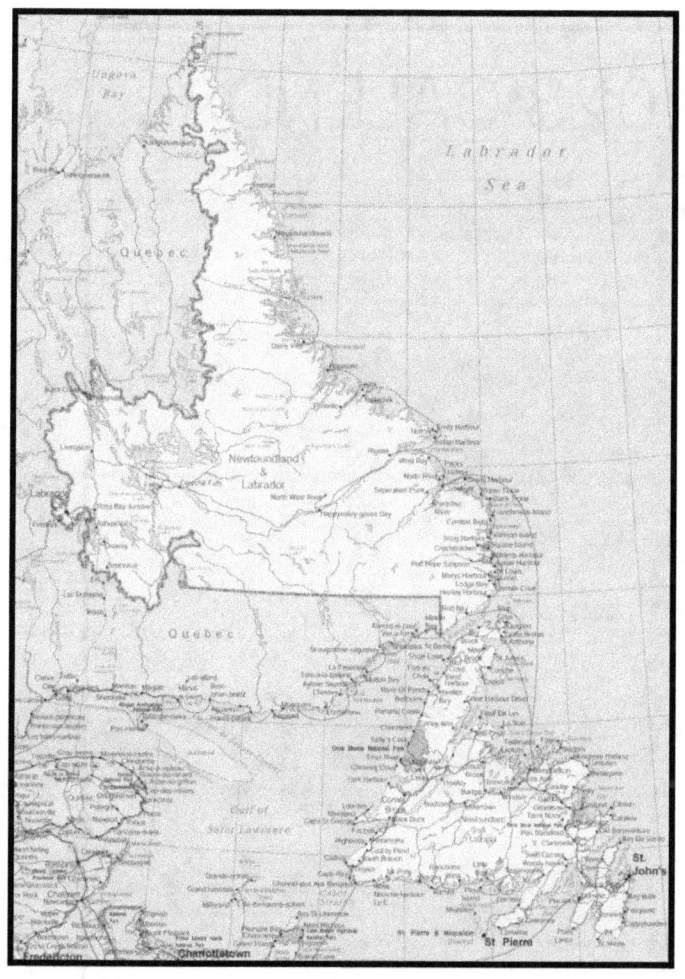

Calendars

2023 CALENDAR

JANUARY
S	M	T	W	T	F	S
1	2	3	4	5	6	7
8	9	10	11	12	13	14
15	16	17	18	19	20	21
22	23	24	25	26	27	28
29	30	31				

FEBRUARY
S	M	T	W	T	F	S
			1	2	3	4
5	6	7	8	9	10	11
12	13	14	15	16	17	18
19	20	21	22	23	24	25
26	27	28				

MARCH
S	M	T	W	T	F	S
			1	2	3	4
5	6	7	8	9	10	11
12	13	14	15	16	17	18
19	20	21	22	23	24	25
26	27	28	29	30	31	

APRIL
S	M	T	W	T	F	S
						1
2	3	4	5	6	7	8
9	10	11	12	13	14	15
16	17	18	19	20	21	22
23	24	25	26	27	28	29
30						

MAY
S	M	T	W	T	F	S
	1	2	3	4	5	6
7	8	9	10	11	12	13
14	15	16	17	18	19	20
21	22	23	24	25	26	27
28	29	30	31			

JUNE
S	M	T	W	T	F	S
				1	2	3
4	5	6	7	8	9	10
11	12	13	14	15	16	17
18	19	20	21	22	23	24
25	26	27	28	29	30	

JULY
S	M	T	W	T	F	S
						1
2	3	4	5	6	7	8
9	10	11	12	13	14	15
16	17	18	19	20	21	22
23	24	25	26	27	28	29
30	31					

AUGUST
S	M	T	W	T	F	S
		1	2	3	4	5
6	7	8	9	10	11	12
13	14	15	16	17	18	19
20	21	22	23	24	25	26
27	28	29	30	31		

SEPTEMBER
S	M	T	W	T	F	S
					1	2
3	4	5	6	7	8	9
10	11	12	13	14	15	16
17	18	19	20	21	22	23
24	25	26	27	28	29	30

OCTOBER
S	M	T	W	T	F	S
1	2	3	4	5	6	7
8	9	10	11	12	13	14
15	16	17	18	19	20	21
22	23	24	25	26	27	28
29	30	31				

NOVEMBER
S	M	T	W	T	F	S
			1	2	3	4
5	6	7	8	9	10	11
12	13	14	15	16	17	18
19	20	21	22	23	24	25
26	27	28	29	30		

DECEMBER
S	M	T	W	T	F	S
					1	2
3	4	5	6	7	8	9
10	11	12	13	14	15	16
17	18	19	20	21	22	23
24	25	26	27	28	29	30
31						

2024

January
MO	TU	WE	TH	FR	SA	SU
1	2	3	4	5	6	7
8	9	10	11	12	13	14
15	16	17	18	19	20	21
22	23	24	25	26	27	28
29	30	31	1	2	3	4

February
MO	TU	WE	TH	FR	SA	SU
29	30	31	1	2	3	4
5	6	7	8	9	10	11
12	13	14	15	16	17	18
19	20	21	22	23	24	25
26	27	28	29	1	2	3

March
MO	TU	WE	TH	FR	SA	SU
26	27	28	29	1	2	3
4	5	6	7	8	9	10
11	12	13	14	15	16	17
18	19	20	21	22	23	24
25	26	27	28	29	30	31

April
MO	TU	WE	TH	FR	SA	SU
1	2	3	4	5	6	7
8	9	10	11	12	13	14
15	16	17	18	19	20	21
22	23	24	25	26	27	28
29	30	1	2	3	4	5

May
MO	TU	WE	TH	FR	SA	SU
29	30	1	2	3	4	5
6	7	8	9	10	11	12
13	14	15	16	17	18	19
20	21	22	23	24	25	26
27	28	29	30	31	1	2

June
MO	TU	WE	TH	FR	SA	SU
27	28	29	30	31	1	2
3	4	5	6	7	8	9
10	11	12	13	14	15	16
17	18	19	20	21	22	23
24	25	26	27	28	29	30

July
MO	TU	WE	TH	FR	SA	SU
1	2	3	4	5	6	7
8	9	10	11	12	13	14
15	16	17	18	19	20	21
22	23	24	25	26	27	28
29	30	31	1	2	3	4

August
MO	TU	WE	TH	FR	SA	SU
29	30	31	1	2	3	4
5	6	7	8	9	10	11
12	13	14	15	16	17	18
19	20	21	22	23	24	25
26	27	28	29	30	31	1

September
MO	TU	WE	TH	FR	SA	SU
26	27	28	29	30	31	1
2	3	4	5	6	7	8
9	10	11	12	13	14	15
16	17	18	19	20	21	22
23	24	25	26	27	28	29
30	1	2	3	4	5	6

October
MO	TU	WE	TH	FR	SA	SU
30	1	2	3	4	5	6
7	8	9	10	11	12	13
14	15	16	17	18	19	20
21	22	23	24	25	26	27
28	29	30	31	1	2	3

November
MO	TU	WE	TH	FR	SA	SU
28	29	30	31	1	2	3
4	5	6	7	8	9	10
11	12	13	14	15	16	17
18	19	20	21	22	23	24
25	26	27	28	29	30	1

December
MO	TU	WE	TH	FR	SA	SU
25	26	27	28	29	30	1
2	3	4	5	6	7	8
9	10	11	12	13	14	15
16	17	18	19	20	21	22
23	24	25	26	27	28	29
30	31	1	2	3	4	5

www.ingramcontent.com/pod-product-compliance
Lightning Source LLC
Chambersburg PA
CBHW071437080526
44587CB00014B/1890